A Leaders guide to

Lean
Presentations

Create outstanding presentations

with

Lean and 6-sigma

LG2LPF507:ISBN 978-0-9932504-3-9

Lean Presentations

Alan Sarsby

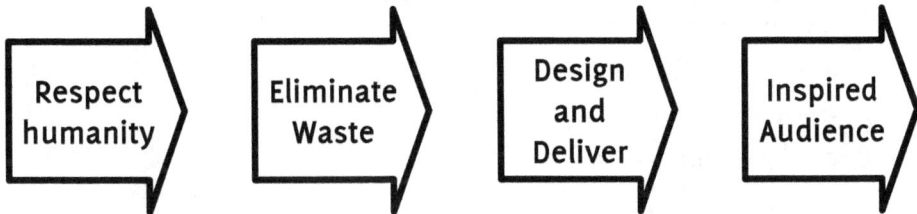

First printing: December 2017
Language <en-gb>
ISBN 978-0-9932504-3-9

The Leadership Library is an imprint of Spectaris Limited.
Registered in England: 05448422

www.leadership-library.co.uk

Forward

The Leader's Guide to Lean Presentations

This is a very innovative application of Lean thinking. How many presentations do you attend which really don't pass the 'does this add value' test? Does the presentation flow naturally? What is the cost of a poor quality presentation?

This book and Alan's associated masterclass workshops help you think about presentations in a totally different way. He provides a comprehensive framework to create effective presentations based on well-established Lean principles.

Alan has combined his extensive knowledge of presentation skills together with a deep understanding of what really engages with audiences. You will see the influence from his mastery of imagery — amongst other things, Alan is an experienced photographer, and shares his knowledge through workshops for camera clubs and photographic societies.

I believe that you will find this handbook is which won't end up forever on the bookshelf. I think you'll go back and refer to it many times, as and when you need a refresher on presentation preparation and delivery.

I certainly will!

Martin Brenig-Jones
Lean Six Sigma Master Black Belt and Coach.
MD, Catalyst Consulting Ltd

Co-author of Lean Six Sigma for Dummies and Lean Six Sigma for Leaders.

Preface

The human race has been described as the compulsive communicator. No other creature has our range of communications abilities — to read, to write, to speak, to gesture. Yet, despite these natural talents, giving a presentation remains a daunting task to many.

There's an old Yorkshire saying which (translated from the vernacular) goes:

If you've nothing to say, say nothing

We've all sat through presentations waiting for the content that never came. These content-free presentations are simply dreadful. Just hot air and a waste of electrons powering the projector; their only contribution is to global warming. Content is important. When you have something to say, then devote your attention to saying it.

Imagine you've been invited to listen to a presentation — unless you're cynical, you don't expect to be treated like an idiot, become bored, or be insulted. The exact opposite is more likely. The audience is your best friend — they want you to succeed, they want a positive experience.

Find out what their needs and expectations are; discover their starting point, and what jargon you must use and which is best avoided. Invest in the audience and they'll pay you back with interest. (And yes, the pun was intended.)

Imagine listening to your own presentation — ask yourself, after this presentation, what will I know, think, feel, or do? If you draw blanks to these questions it's likely to be a worthless presentation.

Presentations need structures because rambles are frustrating to listen to. Even shaggy dog stories have a structure. Structures hold the whole presentation together and keep you and your audience moving in synchronism. A structure is like a map that takes you and your best friends (the audience) on the journey from departure, calling at all the important points, to the destination.

12 Handouts   85

13 Your words   93

14 Working with rogue behaviours   101

15 Get ready — the floor is yours   105

Part 1 — Lean, six-sigma and presentations

1   A Lean presentation?

1.1   Lean and presentations?

Lean and presentations? A quick reaction to Lean and presentations might seem incongruous; but please think again — the Lean philosophy is made up of a single objective and two supporting principles:

Objective: Value to the customer

> The objective in Lean is to deliver value to the customer. The customer is your audience; and they define what is valuable.

Principle: Eliminating waste.

> These improvement activities are characterised by systematic and logical processes with a relentless focus on measurement-based analysis, leading to process and efficiency improvements.

Principle: Respect for humanity

> It is here that the application of the Lean techniques can make a huge difference to your performance as a presenter. Your audience is made up of humans, who are members of humanity. Respect for humanity covers important aspects of a presentation: respect for your audience's time, respect for what they already know, and respecting the fact that your audience came to your presentation to gain something valuable.

Applying both principles: eliminating presentation wastes, and respect for humanity, the Lean toolkit is a means to design a valuable presentation from the outset.

Expanding these to include the classic representations of Lean leads to four top-level themes. A variation from the usual drawing of Lean is shown in Figure 1.

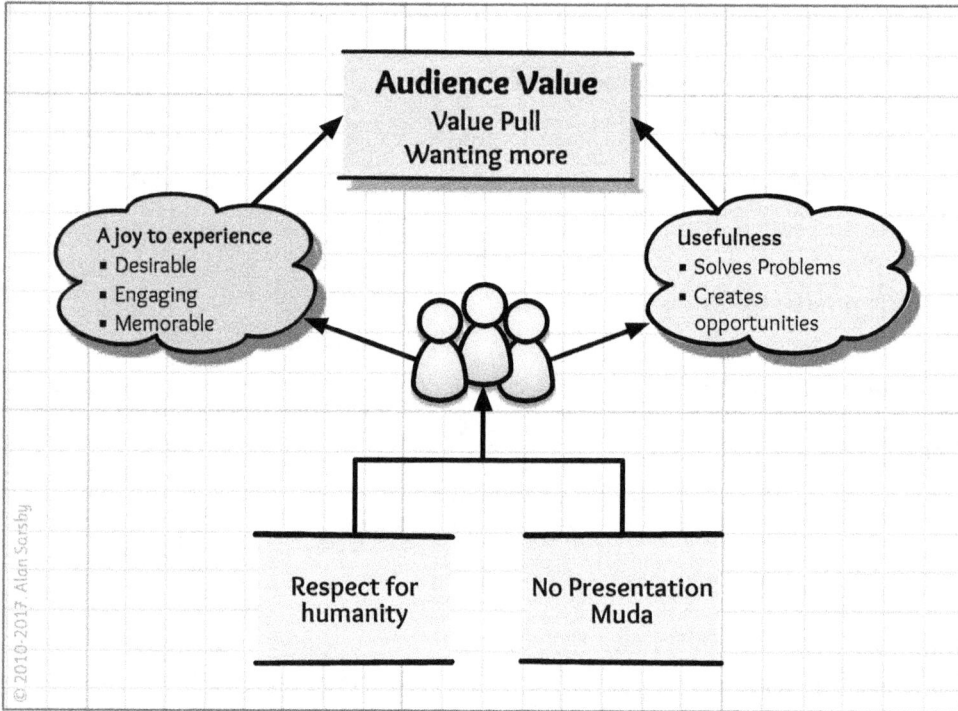

Figure 1: The objective — Value for your audience

1.2   The price of poor quality presentations

There are numerous exaggerations making bold statements such as 40 thousand/ million/whatever, presentations per day somewhere in the world; it is a good headline grabber, but without the rigour of citable academic standards.

Nevertheless one might make a reasonable estimate: In the corporate world, you might go to three meetings per week and sit through three presentations per meeting; in total 9 presentations per week, approximating to 450 presentations per year. If each presentation is 15 minutes, you spend 90 hours listening and watching presentations. Multiply that by your cost of employment and then multiply that by the number of your colleagues and you'll arrive at some staggeringly large lost opportunity cost!

You and your organisation pay a price for poor quality presentations. Some root-causes are shown in Figure 2. Please feel free to add your own.

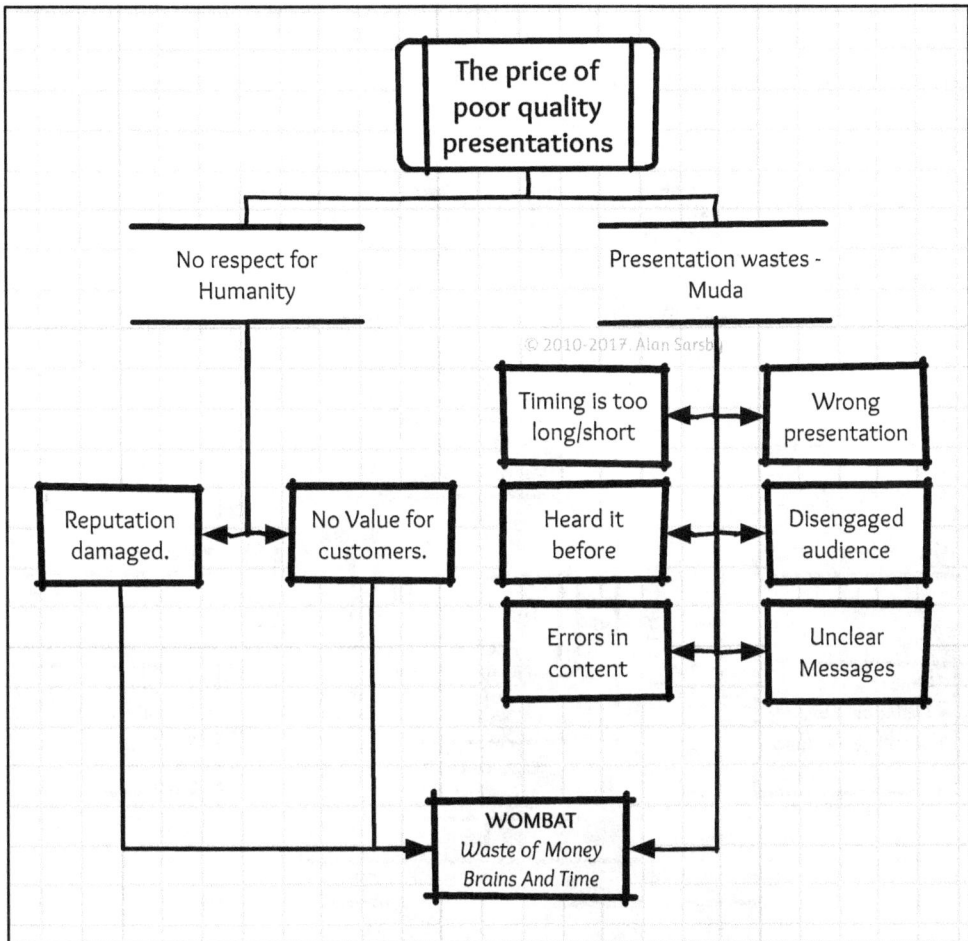

Figure 2: The price of poor quality presentations

1.3   Best and worst presentations

Thinking about some of the best and worst presentations you've enjoyed or endured, and then placing these characteristics on the scorecard-like grid could look something similar to Figure 3. The worsts are presentation wastes. The bests are Critical To Quality (CTQ) factors.

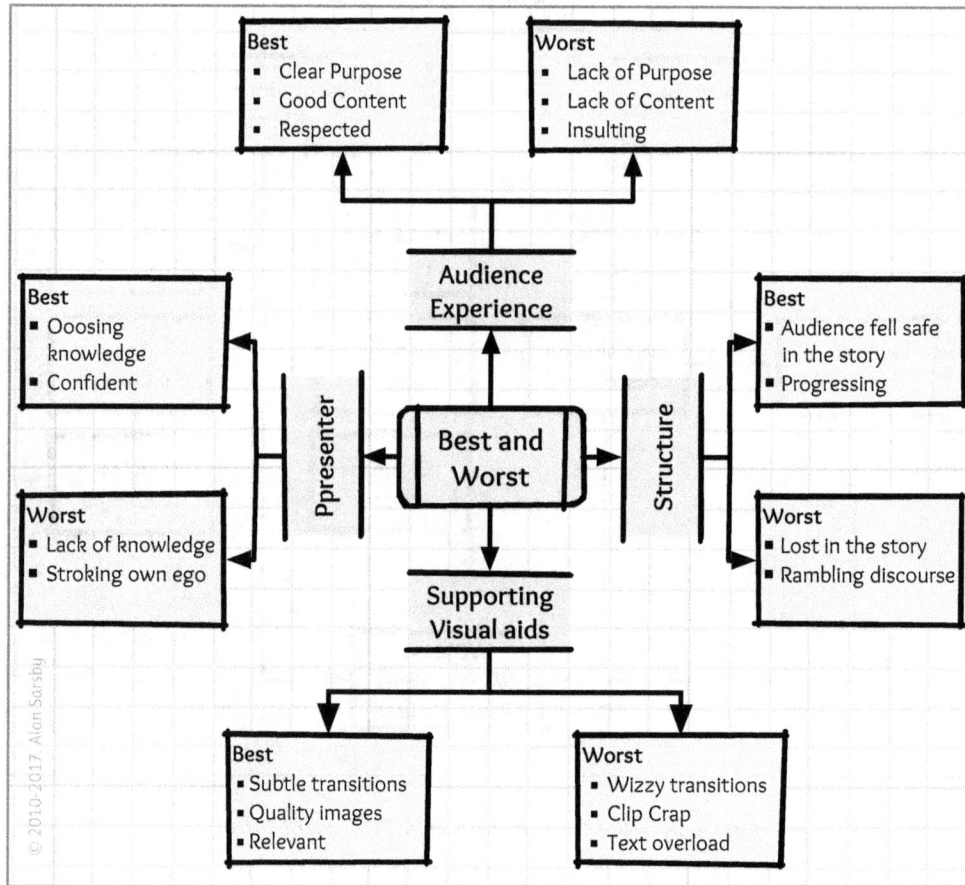

Figure 3: The best and worst presentations

2 Map the value flow

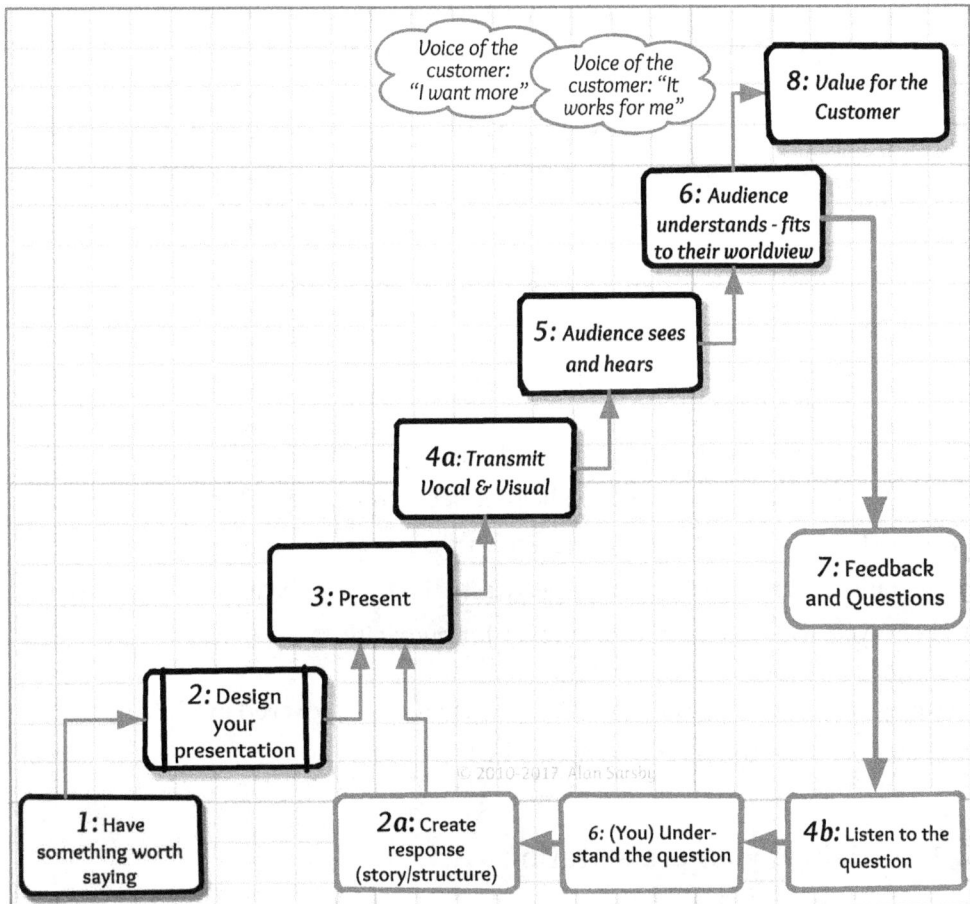

Figure 4: Mapping the Value Flow of a presentation

2.1 A value flow

In the Lean methodology, mapping the value flow ensures integrity so that actions lead to value for the customer. For a presentation, the value flow is shown in Figure 4.

2.2   Have something worth saying

The beginning of the value flow is to have something worth saying. In quality systems, the goal is to begin with quality because if you don't the quality becomes more difficult to correct as the presentation design progresses. The axiom *Quality First* also applies to presentations. You should also consider whether you need a presentation at all? Would an email or memo suffice?

Having something worth saying avoids the failure mode of having nothing to say then wasting your audience's time saying it: and hence, no respect for humanity.

2.3   Create a structure to carry your message

The second step of the value flow is the creation of a structure to carry your message. Without a structure your messages become lost in logorrhoea[1].

The adage about telling a story is a good one, humans have evolved to pay attention to stories; but is mostly unhelpful because although the advice is given generously, there are few which explain what a story is or how to tell one in a presentation. Badly constructed stories waste time, leave the audience confused, and cost you your reputation; no respect for humanity.

Creating and using stories for business presentations is covered in §5.3 and a resource of story structures is in Appendix 1.

2.4   Deliver your presentation

At this stage in the value flow, you have something to day, your messages clear and organised, and the story structure is in place. It is time to deliver your presentation. Here you are in direct engagement with your audience so your stance and body language, your choice of words, and the quality of your visuals all combine to satisfy your objectives and the audience's needs.

---

1   Logorrhoea
       a) a communication disorder resulting in incoherent talkativeness.
       b) verbosity, speech or writing which uses excessive words.

For many this is the terrifying part; but with good preparation, it is not so much the challenge of knowledge, but a confidence of delivery that makes the presentation successful.

2.5   Transmission from you to the audience

The fourth element in the value flow is transmit what you want to achieve, to the ears and minds of the audience. The main challenge is to manage and control the noise. In telecommunications, this is the signal-to-noise ratio. In art theory, noise is the figure-to-ground ratio. Noise is covered specifically later in this book.

2.6   See and hear

If all is going to plan, your audience can both see and hear you. The vital elements are the acoustics and the line of sight to you. Remember that hearing, listening, and understanding are separate aspects. Hearing is the physiological mechanism where sound waves impinge the eardrum then the hammer and anvil send the waves down the cochlea where tiny hair-like strings are activated by different frequencies, these send signals to the brain. Listening is a cognitive process where the brain decodes the signal into patterns of sound such as words or music. And finally, understanding is a more intense cognitive activity which makes sense of the words resulting in the meaning.

2.7   Audience understanding

The acoustics and visuals might be good, but it does not mean that the audience understands you. Understanding comes through a cognitive activity, and this in turn depends on what you say and how you say it — it is the result of good presentation design. And good presentation design depends on knowing your audience together with clarity of purpose in your objectives.

Knowing your audience and understanding what they know, and what they want to know or need to know, is the underlying critical-to-quality of a presentation.

2.8   Feedback

All good presentations involve feedback. Feedback takes many forms: non-spoken such as smiles and gestures (including grunts, and sighs), spoken feedback such as the question and answer session. And finally the applause of appreciation (or the slow-clap of disapproval).

A well designed and engaging presentation should prevent the negative aspects of feedback, so the one aspect to take care of is questions and answers. If you've been holding your audience's attention, this is a combination of their cognitive processing, forming their question, then transmitting it to you. You then have the job of understanding their question (a cognitive process), formulating a reply (a quick re-run of design) and transmitting it back to the audience questioner.

2.9   Value in the eyes of the your audience

All of which leads us to the primary goal of value for the customer. There are many types of value, and it would be foolish to pick just one; a reasonable assumption is that at each audience member has a different expectation of value. Value can be designed-in to a presentation. At its simplest, you could ask (and hence test): was it useful to the audience? What could they do, achieve, or change following your presentation?

Part 2 — Designing presentations using Lean

3 Design principles for presentations

3.1 General principles

The six design principles following appear on three occasions in this work: once for application to the whole presentation, again for the design of slides, and finally for the design of handouts.

Design principle 1 — Purpose. The presentations, including the slides and handouts, must have a purpose. Without a purpose the presentation is a Lean waste: eliminate it!

Design principle 2 — Fit to the audience. Adapt the content to match your audience. For example the vocabulary and jargon, building on what they already know. Hence, you must understand your audience.

Design principle 3 — Content to noise[1] ratio. The content is the message, idea, or purpose; noise is anything that is not relevant or distracts from that purpose. Only give a presentation if it has a purpose; only put an object on a slide if it has a need to be there, and only create a handout if it's needed.

Design principle 4 — Story arc. Your whole prese ntation is supported by a story arch, see §5.3 and the example in Figure 10. A slide also needs a story arch, so does a handout.

Design principle 5 — Effective redundancy. The content of the slide, especially text, should be different from the words spoken by you. The words *heard* by the audience, and the words *read* by the audience, reinforce each other hence the effective redundancy.

Design principle 6 — Coherent and consistent. If your presentation and slides are incoherent, the story is lost; if they are inconsistent there is a risk that your audience thinks they're suddenly watching a different presentation.

---

1   In audio and radio engineering the content to noise ratio is known as the signal-to-noise ratio. or the the Q factor. In visual arts it is known as Figure to Ground; Figure is main subject, Ground is everything else. The principles are the same.

3.2 Preparation is everything

Everything starts with preparation. It's likely that you have come across the two phrases: 3 Ps and 5 Ps:

- 3 Ps — Preparation Precedes Performance, and

- 5 Ps — Poor Preparation Precedes Poor Performance or Proper Preparation Prevents Poor Performance.

- There is a longer version, the 7Ps: 'Pretty Poor Preparation Precedes Pretty Poor Performance.' There is also a grittier industrial version!

Preparation is needed at every stage in readiness for a presentation.

Preparation of yourself

Developing the skills and knowledge about training, and the key behaviours of a good trainer, prepares you for the role of training.

Preparation — planning and organising

This includes the planning and organising of training materials, the invitations, the venue, and other logistics.

Preparation to deliver the presentation

Getting ready for the on-the-day training delivery, so you and the participants have a great training event.

If you do only one thing to elevate the state of humanity, don't give pointless, empty, content-free, presentations. Preparation solves all those problems. Thank you.

3.3   Key inputs for presentation design

The key inputs for presentation design are:

Is a presentation needed? Could the subject and purpose be in other forms of communication?

Understand your audience:

- What is the topic or subject matter of the presentation? What is your audience interested in?

- Is the subject/topic relevant to your audience?

- What depth and breadth of treatment is required?

- Clarity of purpose — why this presentation?

- Defining your key messages — what do you want your audience to know, think, or do, as a result of your presentation?

Without these inputs you run the risk of delivering the wastes shown in Figure 2, and not respecting humanity.

Let's assume that a presentation is appropriate, and you've to give it. What next? The Lean principle is 'Value in the eyes of the customer.' For a presentation, this principle means understanding your audience. Remember there are other audience members who are also your customers and value different things. These different types of customer/audience are often known as stakeholders.

> Note: You might have already encountered the advice of avoiding presentation software at the beginning of presentation project; that same advice is repeated here: Switch off your computer and go analogue. Begin your project work in the touch-and-feel mode with a pencil, paper, flip-charts/whiteboards, and sticky notes.

3.4   Value in the eyes of the customer

Many presentations start life with the dual requirement statement of *"... to give a presentation about xyz to the abc"* The *xyz* is the subject matter, and the *abc* is the audience. Because some subject matter is only applicable to specific types of audience, we'll start with that.

In 6σ, this analysis is the territory of the *In the frame/Out of frame* tool. The basic form is shown in Figure 5, which is then expanded into a stakeholder map.

The second tool is an audience analysis tool which is created from the adaptation of other lean tools. In practice there is always iteration between the tools.

3.5   Identifying stakeholders and scope

Stakeholder analysis helps you to tailor your presentation so it has the best chance of satisfying the various groups who are either watching your presentation of have an interest in the outcome.

Developing Figure 5 into a more detailed stakeholder map shown in Figure 6 helps with the Purpose, the Scope, and the needs of other stakeholders such as Public Relations, Brand Managers, and yourself.

3.6   Who is your audience for the presentation?

Each group is likely to have different expectations so it is worth considering who will be on the 'receiving end' of your presentation: With the Inside/Outside the frame tool, Figure 6, and the size and style framework in Figure 7, you are in a good position to formulate a clear purpose, and an associated objective.

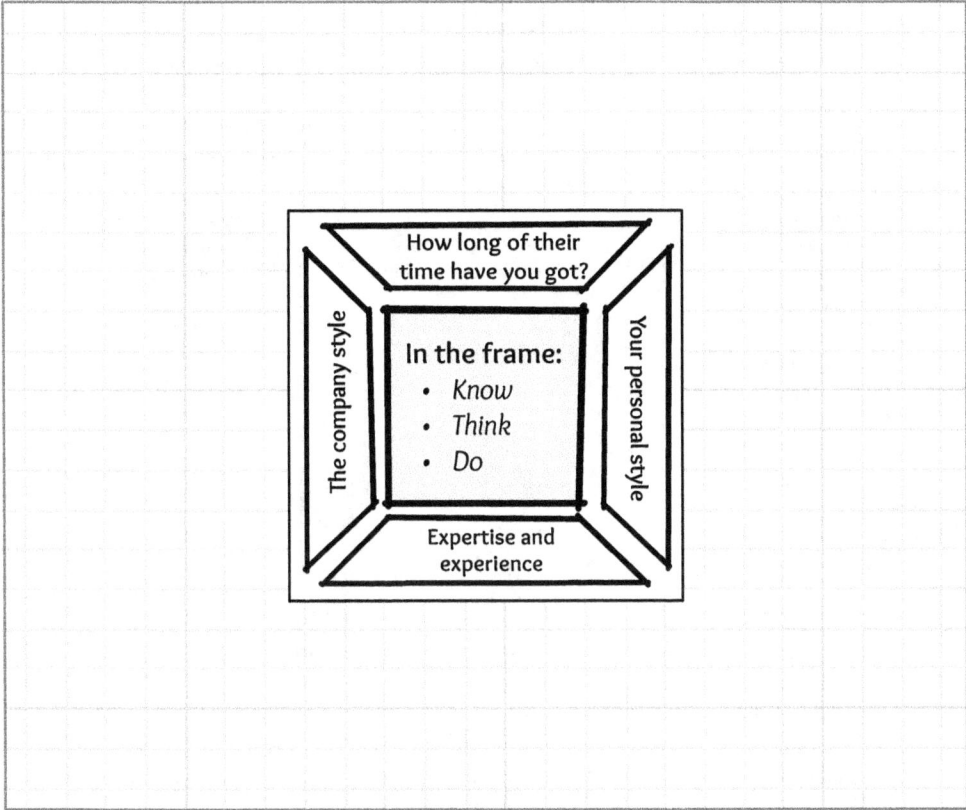

Figure 5: Inside/Outside the frame

The company style

How long of their
time have you got?

Your personal style

In the frame:
- *Know*
- *Think*
- *Do*

Expertise and
experience

Expectations:
- To learn
- To take action

Prior knowledge
- Their seniority
- Their vocabulary

Why are they there?
- Sent/Volunteered
- Paid/Free

Public relations:
- Brand values
- Partner relationships

Marketing objectives:
- New markets
- New opportunities

Why us?
- Be seen as experts
- Be seen as leader

How long of their time have you got?

The company style

Your personal style

In the frame:
- *Know*
- *Think*
- *Do*

Expertise and experience

Your objectives:
- To propose change
- To share, to train

Your expertise:
- Reputation
- Your knowledge

Why you?
- Sent/sponsored
- Asked

Subject matter:
- Expertise
- How to …

Demonstrate
- Challenges
- Solutions

Why us?
- Trust
- Experts

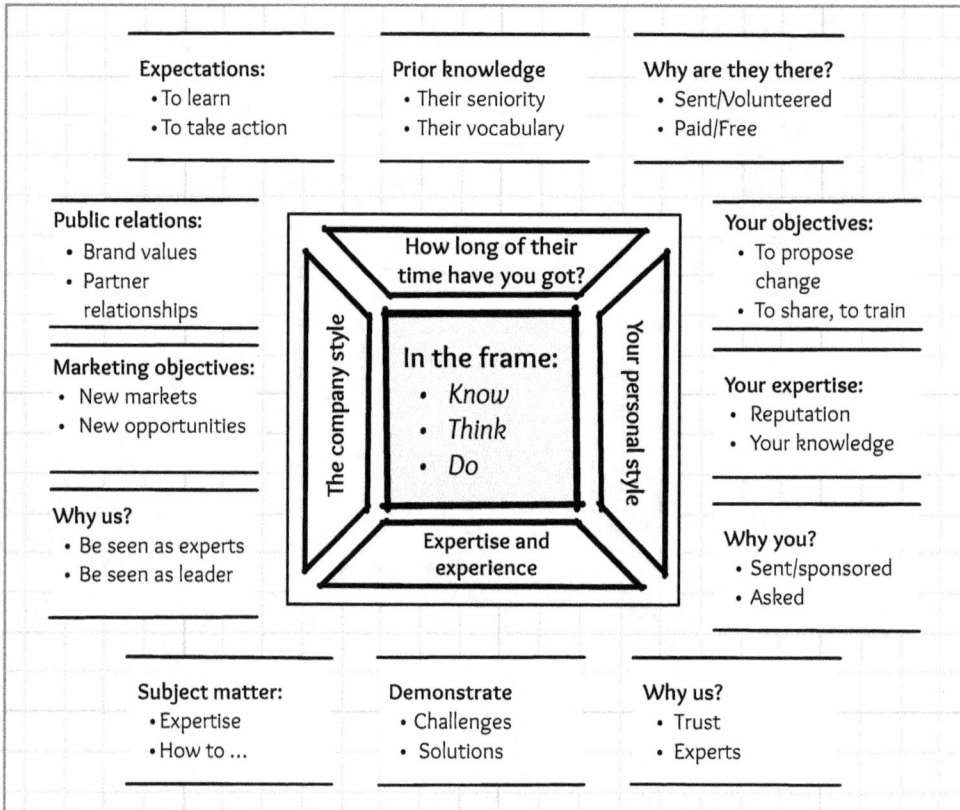

Figure 6: Inside/Outside the frame: as a stakeholder map

Who is your audience

Size	Co-workers	Line management	Technical people	Customer facing (Sales, Marketing)
Small meeting	White board	White board Business subjects	Details, Flowcharts	Features and benefits
Large Seminar	Presentation with visuals	Executive summary	Tools and techniques	Motivations, Key objectives
Lecture	Co-workers don't need a lecture	Lecturing management is a bad idea	How to do 'x'. Technology focus	Check with the client if this is a good fit

© 2010-2017. Alan Sarsby

Style	Co-workers	Line management	Technical people	Customer facing (Sales, Marketing)
Scripted	On screen	Short & sweet. Business case walk through	Business case like with enablers	Features and benefits. Consultative.
Workshop	Small workshop with hands-on involvement.	Strategy workshop.	This is what you have to do.	Hands-on how to do 'x'
Casual	Knowledge transfer.	Check if this is a good match.	Theory then practical	How to ..

Figure 7: Audience size and style analysis

4 Have something worth saying

4.1   Purpose

Our first step in Figure 4 is to have something worth saying. This is achieved by being clear about three factors:

Answer the 'why'

> Pose the question "why am I doing this presentation?" Frame this in the style of a business case. In the example of Figure 8, the business case is to generate new business and to elevate their reputation so they are seen as experts in the subject. The answer to this *'why'* is an internal consideration and not exposed to your audience.

The purpose

> A purpose is the reason that you are giving a presentation at all. The purpose should answer the *'What'* element: in the example the 'what' is 'to pitch the training catalogue'. It might help to regard the purpose as the input consideration. Using the purpose is a good way of starting a presentation.

The objective

> The objective is the *'desired output'* or 'desired result' statement. In Figure 8, the desired result is 'to gain a follow-up meeting'.
> The objective is also an internal consideration and not exposed to your audience.

Without a purpose, your presentation has nothing to contribute. You would be creating waste and in contempt of the Respect for humanity principle.

A well-formed purpose is the first step of designing and delivering a great presentation. Some suggestions are shown in Table 1.

Table 1: Examples of a purpose

	Giving information	Giving a pitch	Knowledge Transfer	Acts of Leadership
Purpose	• Updates • News • Sales offers • Promotion campaigns • Give permission/ authorisation • Give advice • Share an experience	• To respond to a requirement • Request permission to... • Invitations • Request information or proposals • Request help • Request authority	• To fulfil a training need • To share knowledge • To demonstrate a widget ... • To close the gap between knowing and doing • To elevate the participants' skills	• To motivate and encourage • Share successes • Announcements • Changes • To set direction • To release the past • To meet a new challenge • To lead a celebration

A good test of a well-formed purpose statement is to read it aloud. For example: speak aloud the partial sentence below with the gaps completed:

"The purpose of this presentation is to   ...   ."

Examples:

> *"The purpose of this presentation is to describe the plan for this autumn's product promotion, together with the campaign bonus scheme, so we can all enjoy a successful quarter "*

> *"The purpose of this presentation is to introduce the basic controls of an oscilloscope so you can observe and measure a waveform."*

> *"The purpose of this session in today's project management training is to provide you with tools and techniques to protect your project from hidden, and possibly hostile, stakeholders."*

> *"The purpose of this presentation is to propose a solution to the xyz problem."*

"I'd like to give you an update on the first three months' progress of our xyz project."

"My short talk this morning is to demonstrate why our key operational machine is slowly drifting out of tolerance - and costing £000s per day in uncontrolled maintenance."

> Note —the purpose statement is much stronger if you conclude it with a benefit.

Using a purpose, as a statement of intention, is also a great way to start a presentation by setting your audience's expectations and synchronising them with the content they are about to hear.

4.2   Value for the customer: The Audiences' — expectations

Imagine that you are to attend a presentation, what would make it good for you?

The absence of the muda or disrespect factors in Figure 2 would be good, and hopefully you'd like more of the 'best' factors in Figure 3.

The best factors come in two forms:

- The rational and logistical — clarity of slides, audibility, start and finish on time.

- Factors relating to the *experience* of the presentation.
  This is the humanistic — respect for humanity — aspect of your presentation; it is what separates you from a robot delivering the same material!

> If you have studied Kano's[1] theory of customer satisfaction, you might recognise these as the one-dimensional (also known as linear requirements) drivers of satisfaction, and the exciters or delighters. A third category is the distractors: those are the presentation wastes.

---

1   Professor Noriaki Kano. See, for example, en.wikipedia.org/wiki/Noriaki_Kano/

4.3   Presentation charter

In Lean and six-sigma, a commonly used tool is the project charter. A presentation is a project, and creating a presentation charter is a useful means to clarify:

- Why you are doing a presentation — the main points in the style of a business case summary.

- The purpose — what the presentation is about and its scope.

- The objectives/results — what you want as a consequence of the presentation.

An example is in Figure 8 following.

Why	Purpose	Objective
• New business development • Extend Reputation	To pitch our training catalogue.	To gain a follow-up meetings with prospects.

In/Out Scope	Key messages	Timeline
Training only, not consultancy	• Training is good for you • We're experts. • We're great to work with.	30 minute slot on 23 June.

Team:	Presenters: Jenny Martin	On the day support: Mark Lynda

Figure 8: Presentation Charter - template with example

5   Presentation design

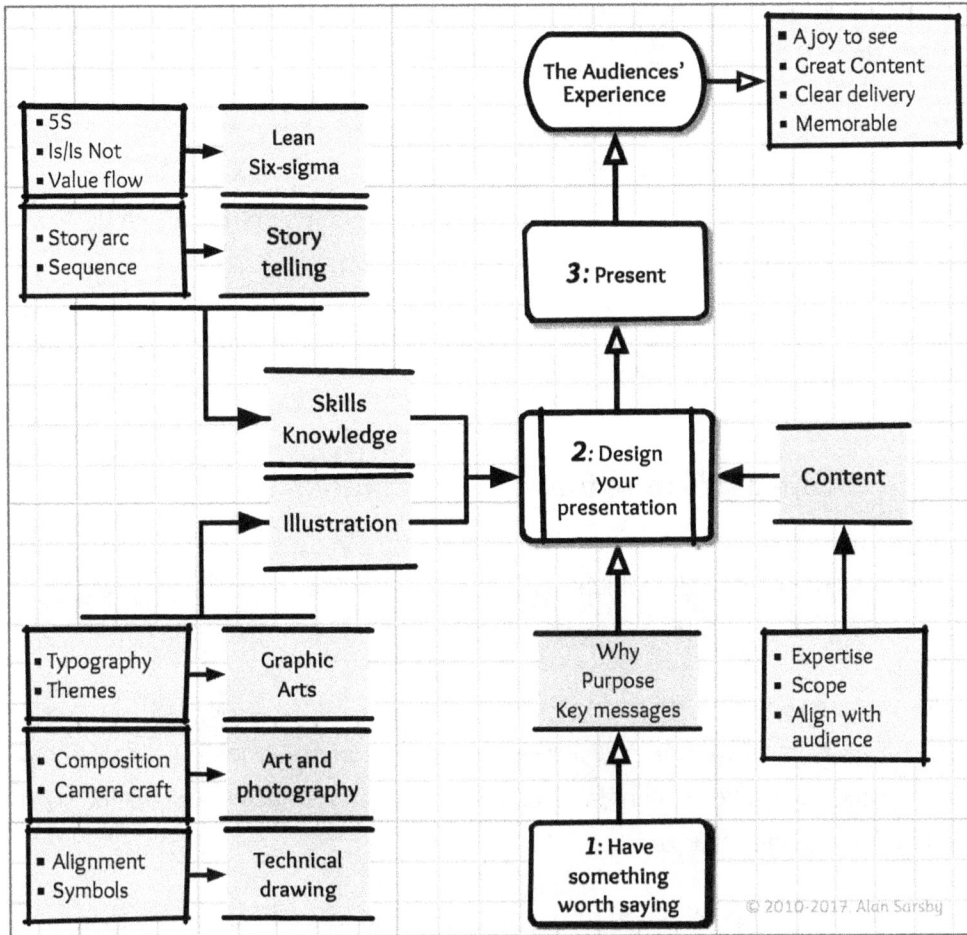

Figure 9: The inputs for step 2: Designing the presentation

5.1   The need for design

Design is the act of working out how to create something from inputs such as objectives, specifications, or aims and desires. Design is part of many aspects of human endeavour. Design is in architecture, engineering, and as you might have guessed, in presentations. Poor quality presentations are often the result of missing out the design.

The overall design for presentations is in Figure 4 where it is performing the job of mapping the 'value flow'. The first part of the design was covered in §4 (step 1 in Figure 4 and again in Figure 9). Step 1 delivered presentation charter with the 'why', 'purpose', and 'what' so that you have something to say.

This second step brings together the various tools, skills, and knowledge to design a great presentation.

5.2   Create a structure for your presentation

An important aspect of designing presentations is to create a structure. A structure is a set of placeholders into which you put words and visuals to convey your message to your audience.

Structures are even more important to your audience because they don't know what they are about to hear. A structure helps the audience synchronise the purpose and points, helps them take notes, helps them to place your idea into their internal knowledge schema.

A good structure also helps you to stay on-topic, and to avoid confusing loopbacks that interrupt the flow.

A structure is a story. The whole presentation is a story, made up of a series of connected stories, similar to the chapters in a book.

5.3   What is a story?

Common advice is to tell stories, but what is a story? There is no single good definition and the definitions varies depending on your topic and your audience. A story includes some or all of:

- A situation or an environment within which an opportunity or problem exists. (Sometimes known as the premise.)

- Within the situation, what is the opportunity, the problem, or the conflict?

- The Impact of the opportunity or problem.

- Characters: the classic characters are protagonists, antagonists, and a narrator.

  - A hero: the protagonist — who owns the problem or opportunity and makes the difficult leadership decisions.

  - A villain: the antagonist who creates problems or obstacles. (Including enemies, competitors, regulators, and so on.)

  - A narrator who provides a commentary or voice-over to link scenes or elements to move the story forward.
    In classic literature the three characters are real people, however they don't need to be, and in business presentations are frequently inanimate objects. For example a faulty machine is the antagonist in the story about restoring a problematic machine to its operating tolerance.

- A resolution: The problem is fixed, or the opportunity is seized.

- A denouement: wrapping up the loose ends.

A story is a structure to carry your audience through the points and deliver the purpose of your presentation. For the most part, the story is invisible to your audience, because the audience are inside the story, aligning with the characters.

The *is/is not* framework is applied in Table 2 as a summary for stories in presentations.

Table 2: Understanding a story in a presentation

	A Presentation Story Is	A Presentation Story Is Not	Therefore (Design input)	Value for customer
Why	Relevant to support a point	A story is not to fill up space	What story would support the point?	Hmm, this could work for me.
What	Short, to the point	Is not a novel. Not long-winded	Structure	Easy to align with
When	In its logical sequence	Is not separate from the goals.	The whole presentation is a story.	Easy to re-tell to others.
Where	Delivered within the presentation	Is not randomly placed	Story is navigation.	Audience—know where they are.
Who	Protagonist, Antagonist, Narrator.	Is not character overload	Define the characters	Each audience relates to a character
How	Spoken by a character	Is not a third party	Multiple interlocking stories	Believable

© 2010-2016 Alan Sarsby

5.4   Story telling is a structure

Telling stories is where you design the sequence of moments, a structure that conveys your idea to the audience. The storytelling framework is commonly known as the story arc; one such arc is shown in Figure 10 — there are many to choose from, see Appendix 1.

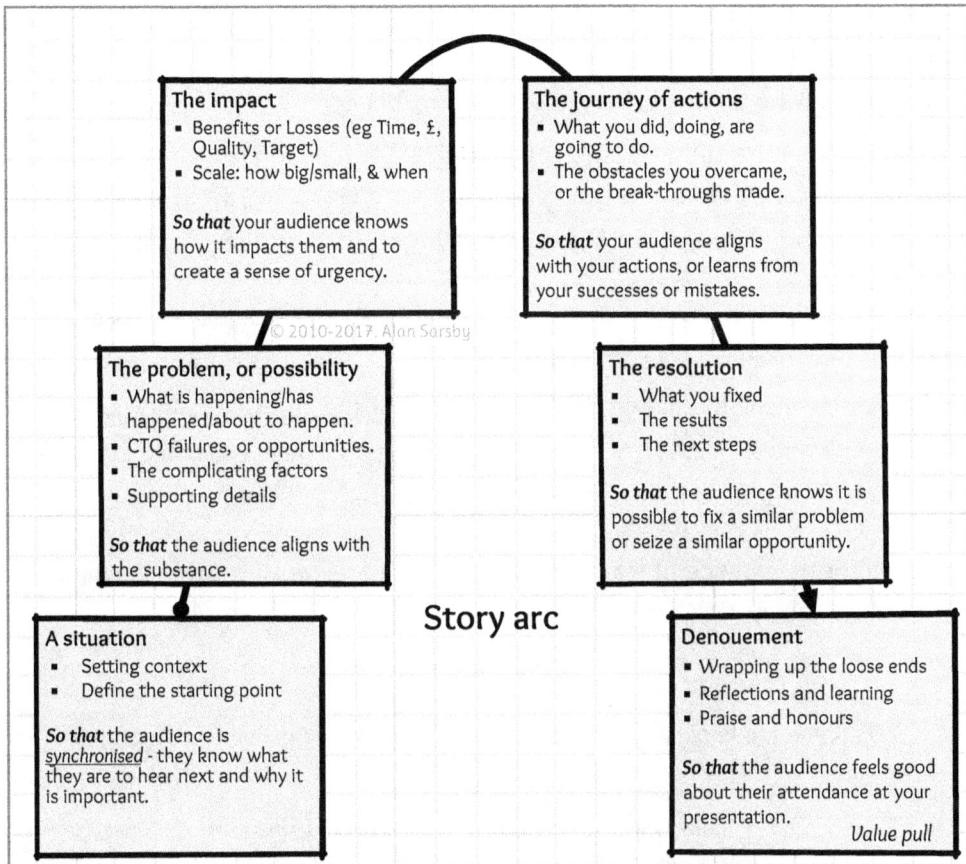

The impact
- Benefits or Losses (eg Time, £, Quality, Target)
- Scale: how big/small, & when

So that your audience knows how it impacts them and to create a sense of urgency.

The journey of actions
- What you did, doing, are going to do.
- The obstacles you overcame, or the break-throughs made.

So that your audience aligns with your actions, or learns from your successes or mistakes.

© 2010-2017, Alan Sarsby

The problem, or possibility
- What is happening/has happened/about to happen.
- CTQ failures, or opportunities.
- The complicating factors
- Supporting details

So that the audience aligns with the substance.

The resolution
- What you fixed
- The results
- The next steps

So that the audience knows it is possible to fix a similar problem or seize a similar opportunity.

Story arc

A situation
- Setting context
- Define the starting point

So that the audience is synchronised - they know what they are to hear next and why it is important.

Denouement
- Wrapping up the loose ends
- Reflections and learning
- Praise and honours

So that the audience feels good about their attendance at your presentation.
Value pull

Figure 10: An example of a story arc template

5.5   Adult learning

All presentations involve an element of learning. Unfortunately, some adults carry historical impediments to their learning: ironically, it is education. The presentations you saw at college had the purpose of education: to learn a curriculum with the objective of examination success[1].

Education and adult learning are different. This is an important distinction because it affects how you and your audience interact, it affects your assumptions, and attitudes about the audience. Treating an adult audience as children is disrespectful and has significant consequences: Adults can and do walk out of presentations, they can fight back, and can certainly damage your reputation. To avoid the pitfalls, it is worth knowing the basics of the theory. But first the jargon:

Pedagogy and Andragogy — The term for the science of education is *pedagogy* — roughly meaning *child leading*. The relationship is that of a knowledgeable parent guiding a child. Children don't yet know how the knowledge they are learning might be applied. Hence the goal of a good teacher is to make every subject interesting, even if the child is without intrinsic motivation.

The term for the science of learning by adults is *andragogy* — roughly meaning *man leading*. The Malcolm Knowles[2] theory of adult learning is based on six presuppositions: all impact on the design of presentations.

- Adults need to know *why* they are learning; hence the importance of a purpose or a benefit.
- Experience (including mistakes) is the basis for learning activities.
- Adults are responsible for their decisions regarding learning.
- Adults are most interested in learning matters that have immediate relevance.
- Learning is by problem solving.
- Adults respond better to internal motivators (self-interest — what is in it for them), rather than external motivators (for example punishment, or lack of punishment).

---

1   If you are involved in adult training, see also the companion work A leader's guide to Training Delivery.

2   Knowles, M. S. (1970, 1980) The Modern Practice of Adult Education. Andragogy versus pedagogy,

The impact of Knowles theory is in both sequence and content.

- In your story-arc, the opening parts should introduce the purpose, relevance, and potential benefits of the subject matter. This satisfies the Knowles andragogic requirement for an adult to know *why* they should be paying attention to your presentation.

- The story arc should include experiences and learning (yours and theirs) so they can align with the points.

- Adults own their learning and actions, so build in summaries, and 'what next' elements.

- If you can, the story arc should include a problem-solving element. This can take several forms. An on-screen puzzle (a great chance to engage with the audience) through to a workshop exercise (great if your audience are arranged in cabaret style seating).

The story arc is an essential design tool in a well-formed presentation.

5.6   Not all stories are presentation stories

Not all stories are suitable for use in a presentation, even if they contain the components in Figure 10.

Unsuitable-stories include: a replay of a conversation, (it is a playback of a dialogue): for example: *"So, I said,   ..., then he said, ...then I said."* This is can be made into the storyline of jokes by adding *"...then I said ... an unexpected twist."*

Citations and reports are not stories: For example, recounting evidence
        "I was proceeding in a westerly direction when I observed the accused...".

Other unsuitable stories include vacation stories, yesterday's football, and anything not relevant to the point you are trying to convey. These are not stories for use in your presentation.

6 Designing engagement

6.1 What is engagement?

Engagement occurs when your audience have become involved in your presentation story, so that they are aligning with a situation, a problem/opportunity, or a character. And then start to think, *"hmm—this applies to me too"* or *"I could do this in my project"* or maybe *"This presenter is great—please come to my team meeting."*

Engagement changes the presentation from a speaker's monologue into a two-way conversation. That conversation might not be spoken aloud, but the engagement is going on inside the heads of your audience. Engagement is an emotional activity — your audience should *feel* engaged. They might not realise it at the time and perhaps only become aware of it later as they recount your presentation to another person.

The foundations for engagement are all the design principles: the value flow, the topic-audience alignment, the 'bests,' and the story structures.

You have no control over the audiences' choice to be engaged or not. But what you can do is to build on the design, and add engagement as a deliberate feature to include engaging moments, or engagement opportunities, into your presentation.

6.2   Engagement techniques

The underlying principle for engagement is to give your audience an activity to perform. Engagement activities include:

Kinaesthetic engagement — ask the audience to perform some task that requires movement, for example a straw poll by a show of hands.

Intellectual engagement — ask the audience to think, reason, or calculate something.

Creative engagement — creating short-duration teams to solve a puzzle or perform some task, and then to give feedback.

Observational engagement — invite the audience to watch something; a video clip or a demonstration.

Quizzical engagement — Ask a rhetorical question that invites the audience to think. For example, *"What's the common thread that joins public health, micro-biology, and the Romans?"*
[Pause for thinking time] *"Yes, you're right, it's Beer!"*

Imaginative engagement — *"Imagine you are a time traveller and you've come back from the thirtieth century. What would you think of public transport?"*

The forgoing ideas are all forms of positive engagement. Negative forms exist, for example:

Risk engagement — *"Last year we had a major safety issue. This week we are being prosecuted. And next month everyone in this room could be in jail for corporate manslaughter."*

> You should also be aware that some very negative forms can be destructive. For example, blame and blaming, inquisitions (whose fault was it), public and ritual humiliations.
> These are not a feature of Lean's principle of Respecting Humanity.

Preparation

To make these techniques work, you'll need to:

- Design a suitable questions or directions.
  Keep these short and simple with a low cognitive load. For example:

  - (Direction) *"Raise your hand* (kinaesthetic) *if you used public transport to get here today"*.

  - (Question) *"Have you ever encountered the situation* (Intellectual) *where your spreadsheet gave you the wrong answer?"*

  - *"In a moment I'll show a short video.* (Direction) *What I'd like you to do is watch* (Observational) *the woman in the green dress and count* (intellectual) *how often she tries to gain the attention of the sales assistant."*

- Think through the likely responses so you are ready to follow up and move the audience along your presentation story arc. For example:

  - *"So should I assume there is a problem with public transport?"* Alternatively, *"Should I assume there is a problem with town-centre parking?"*

  - *"Hmm, so most of you think your spreadsheets give you the right answer! Let me tell you why spreadsheets can't add-up correctly, and then give you four methods to improve spreadsheet reliability."* [1]

  - (Direction)*"Raise your hand if you saw* (Observational) *the customer in the green-dress being ignored; good ... everybody. Now keep your hand in the air* (kinaesthetic) *if she was ignored more than once. And again keep your hand in the air if she was ignored more than five times.* (intellectual) *Ah, yes ... and more than ten times. So what word might you use* (intellectual) *to describe the customer service she experienced. No, No, please don't shout out the rude ones."* [Laughter...]

- For workshop engagements you'll need to design the seating so that a group of people can quickly become a syndicate; and design any materials, for example prompt/task cards for activities.

---

1   This form of engagement uses the principle of cognitive dissonance. The dissonance is between what the audience already believe is true (spreadsheets are accurate) and that you are about to prove that spreadsheets are prone to errors.

7   Noise

7.1   What is noise

Noise is a waste — it is the curse of presentations. Noise can be a very disruptive (and expensive) waste. It wastes your audience's time and patience, and puts your reputation at risk.

Put simply, noise is anything that:

- interferes with your message;

- distracts your audience's attention;

- disrupts your flow; or

- gets in the way, or is not relevant to, the purpose and objective of your presentation.

7.2   The five presentation noises

Noise comes in many forms — audible noise, those the grunts; extraneous content that interferes with the audience's listening and understanding; structural noise (no story arc); theatrical noise — your body doesn't match the message, and visual noise, those dreadful slides.

With so many noises it helps to identify and classify the various forms it can take. Figure 11 illustrates five categories of noise and some approaches for eliminating the noisy wastes.

At every moment during the design, test your work by asking 'does this add or distract?'

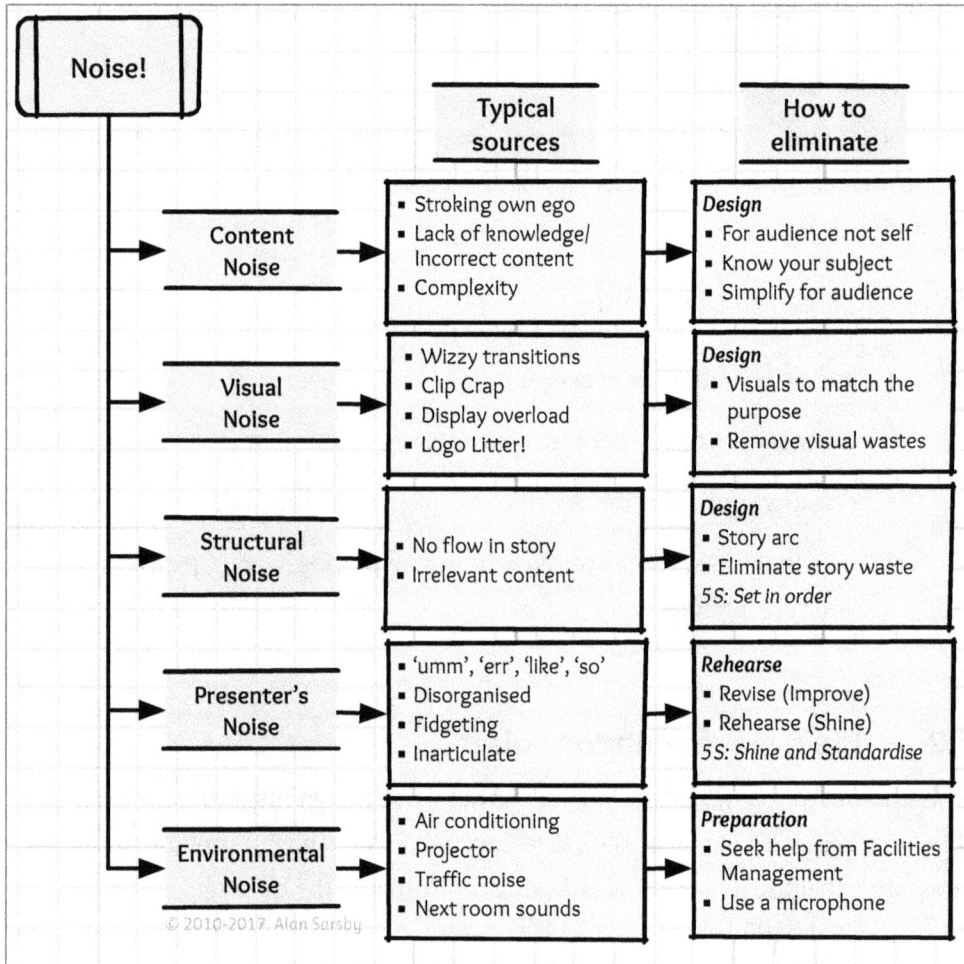

Noise!	Typical sources	How to eliminate
Content Noise	▪ Stroking own ego ▪ Lack of knowledge/ Incorrect content ▪ Complexity	*Design* ▪ For audience not self ▪ Know your subject ▪ Simplify for audience
Visual Noise	▪ Wizzy transitions ▪ Clip Crap ▪ Display overload ▪ Logo Litter!	*Design* ▪ Visuals to match the purpose ▪ Remove visual wastes
Structural Noise	▪ No flow in story ▪ Irrelevant content	*Design* ▪ Story arc ▪ Eliminate story waste *5S: Set in order*
Presenter's Noise	▪ 'umm', 'err', 'like', 'so' ▪ Disorganised ▪ Fidgeting ▪ Inarticulate	*Rehearse* ▪ Revise (Improve) ▪ Rehearse (Shine) *5S: Shine and Standardise*
Environmental Noise	▪ Air conditioning ▪ Projector ▪ Traffic noise ▪ Next room sounds	*Preparation* ▪ Seek help from Facilities Management ▪ Use a microphone

© 2010-2017. Alan Sarsby

Figure 11: Sources and solutions for presentation noise.

Part 3 — Designing slides and visual aids using Lean

8 Principles of Lean Slides

8.1 Lean principles for slides

The same core principles of Lean presentations, introduced in Part 1, are directly applicable to the design of your visual aids — the slides.

Respect for humanity

Perhaps the best measurement of success for a presentation slide is 'a joy to see' With the joy is the ease of understanding the purpose of the slide, and hence learning, so that ultimately an idea or message is conveyed from your head into the heads' of your audience.

Eliminating waste.

Respecting humanity leads directly to the elimination of waste. A waste is anything that interferes with your audiences' ability to read and understand the slide. Visual noise is included in Figure 11, and those points are covered in more detail in the chapters following.

> A slide is a *visual* means of transporting an idea from you to your audience. The goal is to *design* slides so that your audience gain as much as possible FROM your slides; not you trying to put as much as possible ONTO your slides

8.2   Design principles for a slide

The important notion here is that your visual aids, slides, must be *designed* in such a way to meet their purpose. The six-sigma *is/is not* framework, illustrated in Figure 12, analyses the role and function of a slide.

	A Slide Is	A Slide Is Not	Therefore (Design input)	Value for customer
Why	A Relevant *visual* to convey an *idea*	Is not a document	What point is the slide illustrating?	Voice of your customer: *"I understand it"*
What	Focused: the essential points of interest	Not cluttered/ disordered. Not a block of text	Graphic design, Technical drawing, and Art	Easy to align with
When	In its logical sequence	Is not separate from the story.	On display only when required	Easy to re-draw by customer (value pull)
Where	Delivered on-screen	Is not random decoration	All at once, or slow reveal	Audience— guided through the complexity
Who	It's for the audience!	Not a crib sheet for the speaker	Knowledge of the audience	Reduced cognitive load
How	Believable	Not a demanding partner	Sequence and timing	Restrained - pleasing - easy on the eye

Figure 12: A Slide (Projected Image) is/is not analysis

From this six general design principles are:

Design principle 1 — Purpose. The visual aid (slide) must have a purpose. Without a purpose the slide is a waste: eliminate it!

Design principle 2 — Fit to the audience. The slide content must match your audience. For example the vocabulary and jargon, building on what they already know. Hence, you must understand your audience.

Design principle 3 — Content to noise[1] ratio. The content is the message, idea, or purpose; noise is anything that is not relevant or distracts from that purpose. Only put an object on a slide, if it has a need to be there.

Design principle 4 — Story arch for slides. Your whole presentation is supported by a story arch, see §5.3 and the example in Figure 10.
A slide also needs a story arch.

Design principle 5 — Effective redundancy. The content of the slide, especially text, should be different from the words spoken by you. The words *heard* by the audience, and the words *read* by the audience, reinforce the other, hence the effective redundancy.

Design principle 6 — Coherent and consistent. If your slides are incoherent they become lost in the story; if they are inconsistent there is a risk that your audience thinks they're watching a different presentation.

---

1   In audio and radio engineering the content to noise ratio is known as the signal-to-noise ratio. or the the Q factor. In visual arts it is known as Figure to Ground; Figure is main subject, Ground is everything else. The principles are the same.

8.3   Do you need slides?

Starting with the Lean principle of eliminating waste: Do you need slides at all?
Three considerations should help with your decision:

- Is the material difficult to describe solely using the spoken word?

- Is the intention to vary the information channel to the audience?

- Are you are expected to use slides — for example, a sponsor's requirement?

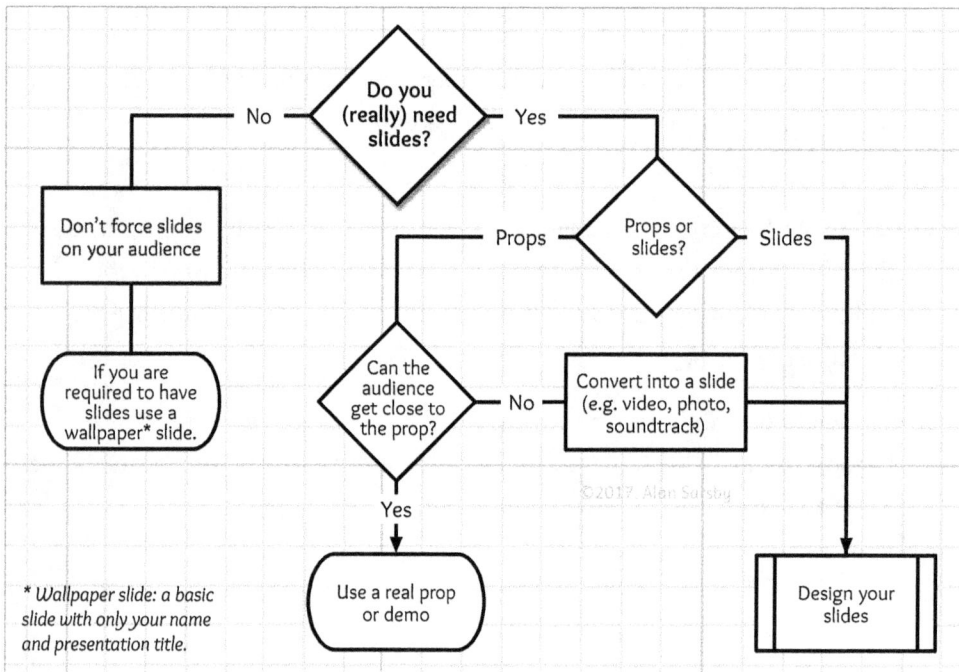

Figure 13: Do you really need slides?

9 Psychology of slide elements

9.1 Chunking

The human mind is an amazing thing, but it has practical limits. Cognitive psychologist George A. Miller[1, 2] researched how much information the brain could hold in working (short-term) memory. This led to the notion of chunking information into small amounts so that the brain can process each without overload.

The interpretation of Miller's research is widely known as the 7 ± 2 rule. That is, the foreground, short term, or working memory holds up to five, and possibly up to nine, chunks. By designing presentations, into chunks (the story arc) or diagrams into fewer component parts, your audience has a greater probability of remembering the information. In the design of training, the learning point is often chunked into no more than four points at once.

A good rule of thumb is that one-slide illustrates one main point. If you need more slides to convey the point use more slides, each adding an extra element to the previous slide. If you need more than one point, keep in mind Miller's chunking rule.

9.2 Picture superiority effect

Humans are visual creatures — our survival and evolution from early apes depended on good vision. Our peripheral vision is more sensitive to movement (a key feature of survival) and our colour perception has evolved to match our natural environment.

---

1   Miller, G. A. (1956). "The magical number seven, plus or minus two: Some limits on our capacity for processing information". Psychological Review. 63 (2): 81–97.

2   See also: https://en.wikipedia.org/wiki/The_Magical_Number_Seven,_Plus_or_Minus_Two.

For presentations, this evolutionary path has led to what is known as the picture superiority effect. A good picture with millions of years of evolutionary advantage beats text every time. Language evolved more recently, and writing systems are a recent invention of only a few thousand years.

If you can, convert your point into a visual; it is more likely to be remembered.

Conversely, a poor-quality slide is likely to disengage your audience. And whilst they are decoding a complex visual, they are excluding your spoken words.

9.3   Gestalt

Gestalt theory[1] is a branch of psychology that considers the mind's perceptions of shape and form. The central theory is that the mind acquires a meaningful perception, and the whole is something other than the sum of its parts.

Objects on a slide have a gestalt relationship with other objects on the slide. This impacts on the visual design of your slide. Some examples of gestalt relationships are:

Proximity — Objects that are close together are perceived as a single entity. For example a horse and its rider. In a flow-chart, a box which is close to its input are perceived as being strongly associated with that input.

Similarity — Objects that are similar, through size, shape, or colour are perceived as belonging together. In the natural world, trees in a wood, are perceived as one forest, rather than several-hundred trees.

Closure — Incomplete objects are finished, or closed, and so perceived as a complete closed object without breaks or gaps in its shape. The brain fills in the missing parts. If your slide contains incomplete graphics, you are forcing the viewer to invest cognitive energy in closing the gaps.

Simplicity — Parallel lines which are close together are perceived as a single line. For example a fence line of, say, three rails or wires, is perceived as a single line. Take care with graphics that trick the mind into simplifying the information (possibly incorrectly).

---

1 Humphrey, G (1924). "The psychology of the gestalt". Journal of Educational Psychology. 15 (7): 401–412]

Continuation — The mind can perceive objects, particularly lines, extending outside the frame. This is useful in the visual arts where the brain can extend the composition beyond image frame. But, a in a graph your audience can continue the line (extrapolate) beyond the slide and possibly draw incorrect conclusions.

Segregation — The mind recognises objects that stand out from the background. The importance for slide design is in contrast. Contrast means segregating the main point (the figure) from its background (the ground).
Designing with segregation/contrast includes for example:

- Taking care that foreground and background colours are separate hues so they don't merge together and become invisible to your audience.

- Keeping the main point of interest uncluttered (refer to §2.5 regarding 'figure-to-ground') so it doesn't become lost. (See also similarity, above.)

Emergence — The mind needs take time to see something that was not apparent at the first viewing. In art this is often expressed as a busy scene within which additional items emerge as a reward for the viewer's investment in looking.

10 Design toolkit for slides

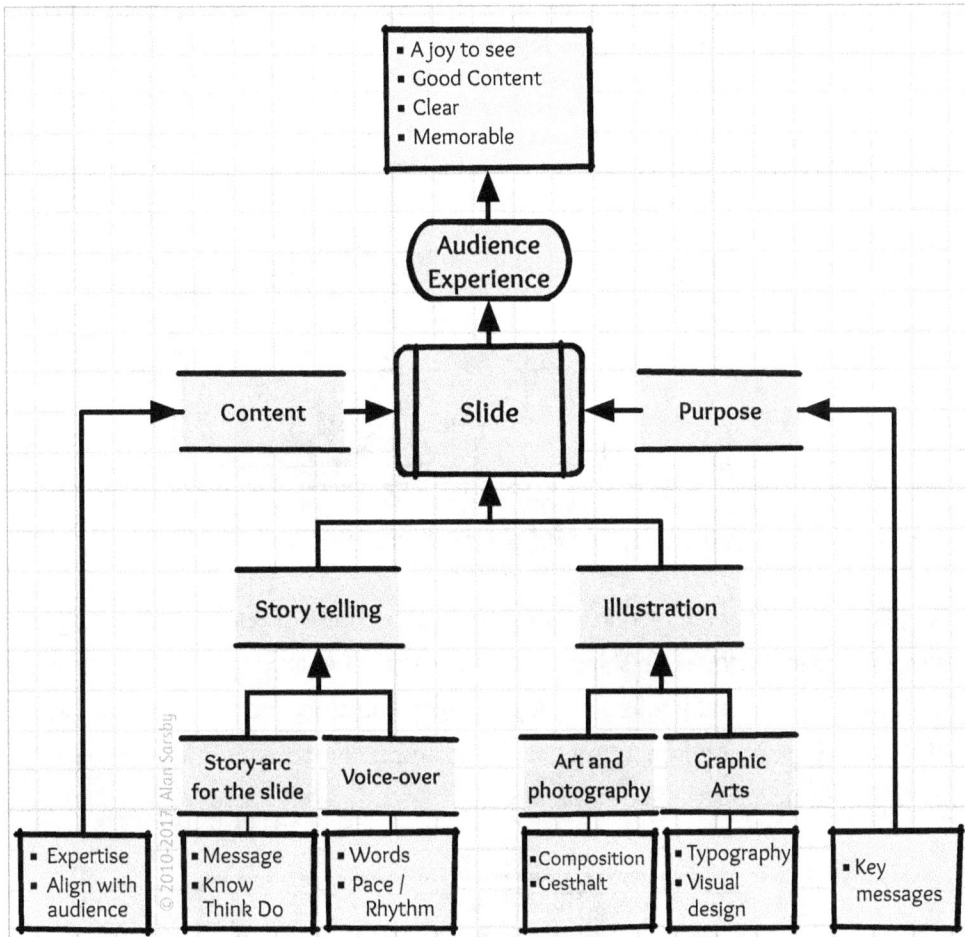

Figure 14: Design toolkit for creating slides.

10.1   Illustration basics

10.1.1   Slides are visual art

Slides are a form of visual art. The illustrative aspect of slide design borrows ideas from the world of art, photography, and graphic design. Among these are:

Composition

The rule of thirds is derived from the golden ratio; the mathematical constant, phi (ɸ). It is a popular composition technique in art and photography. In essence, the view is visually divided into nine rectangular areas as shown in Figure 15. Where the vertical and horizontal lines cross are considered to be where the important aspects or features should be placed.

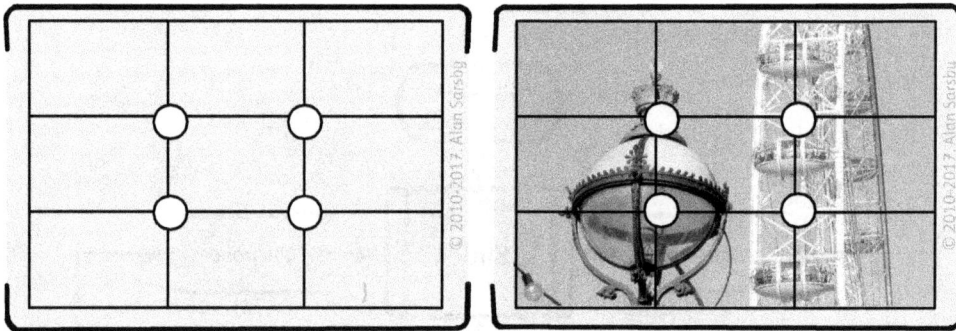

Figure 15: The rule of thirds in slide design.

An application of the rule of thirds grid is to use the bottom-left as the starting point, and the top-right as finishing or destination element.

The viewer's eye naturally follows a beginning to end story motion. This can be useful in story arcs based on a timeline, for example the burning bridge or past-present-future structures. (See Appendix 1.)

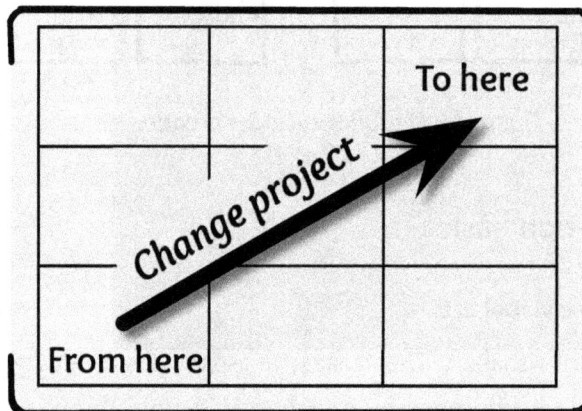

Figure 16: Using the rule of thirds to depict a journey.

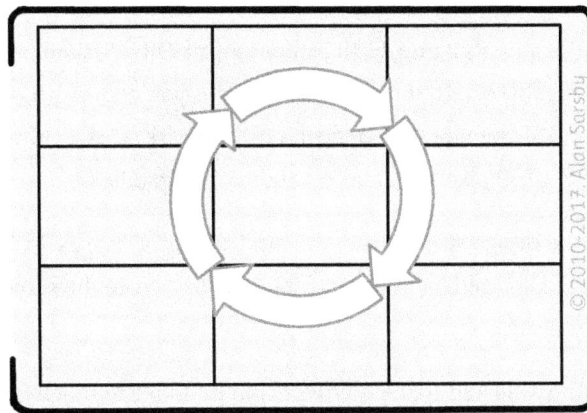

Figure 17: An arrow wheel using the rule of thirds to position the key steps.

Many cameras have a Rule of Thirds grid overlay built in. It is worth experimenting to get the feel for the composition and how this can be applied to slide design and layout.

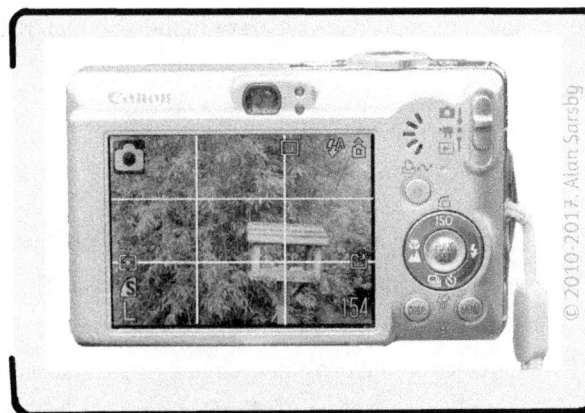

Figure 18: A typical Rule of Thirds overlay on a camera.

10.1.2 Respect the technical limitations

Projected images have inherent limitations. These include:

Low resolution — Despite its name, High Definition, a HD television/projector is only 1920 pixels × 1080 pixels. If it were printed, it is just enough to create a 150mm × 90mm (6″ × 3½″) picture. By contrast a 40″ television, **as a print**, would need 9200 pixels × 6750 pixels. (Approximately 62 Megabytes.)

Limited size — At the design stage, a slide is about the same size as an A4 sheet of paper. Once projected it could be huge, and standing too close the screen you can easily see individual pixels.

Limited space — The available space is limited and putting too much on a slide destroys the figure-to-ground separation. (See §9.3 Gestalt.)

To work within these limitations, you should:

Exercise restraint

It is rare that everything can fit on one slide, so plan multi-slide build-ups.

Keep the visuals simple

If it has to be complex, then produce separate supporting materials.

Keep it BIG and few

A text object benefits from being large.

Line thickness

Use thicker lines — draw your boxes, graphs, and so on with thicker than usual lines. Often the presentation software defaults to 0.75 point. That means the line thickness is about one-hundredth of an inch or 0.26 millimetres. Increase the line thickness so that it is clear on the projector screen. (Presentation software often defaults to measurements in points or pixels; if so choose a line thickness of 3 to 5 points so it becomes visible on the screen.)

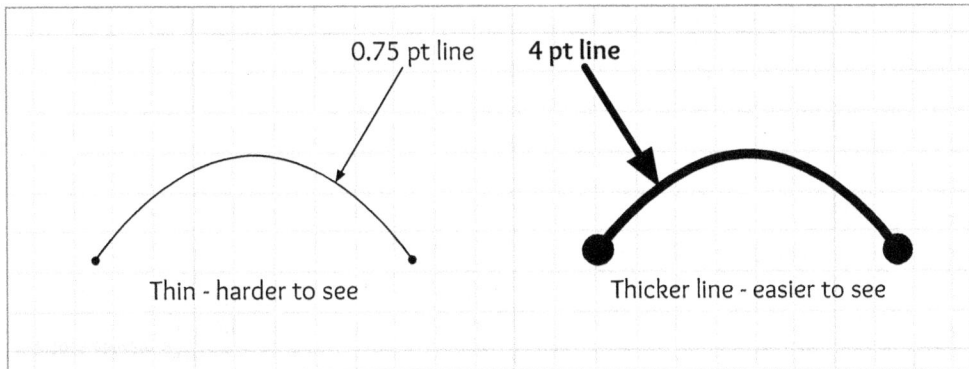

Figure 19: A thicker line is much easier to see on a projected image.

10.1.3   Design with psychology in mind

Complex backgrounds — Complex backgrounds are a distraction, a source of noise. Simple backgrounds work best for projection. Remember too that if you print your slides to paper, a complex background interferes with the content.

Wizzy animations — Our brains have evolved to pay attention to movement. So animations that zigzag around the screen command our attention, and your presentation starts resemble a low-budget television games show.

Avoid visual distractions

Anything that is on-screen (or on-handout) which is not relevant to the learning point, is a distraction.

Common distractions include:

- **Decorative graphics** — for some, the graphic is the first thing they look at. The decoration is the message, and their attention goes to it first.

- **Logo litter** — too many icons become logo-litter (see §11.10 for more detail).

- **Twee graphics** — how many times have you seen the chap with an axe hammering the computer? And that's why you shouldn't use it.

10.1.4 Illustrate one point at a time

Models and processes benefit from a slow reveal form of animation. People who have the theorist learning style[1] appreciate this form of clarity.

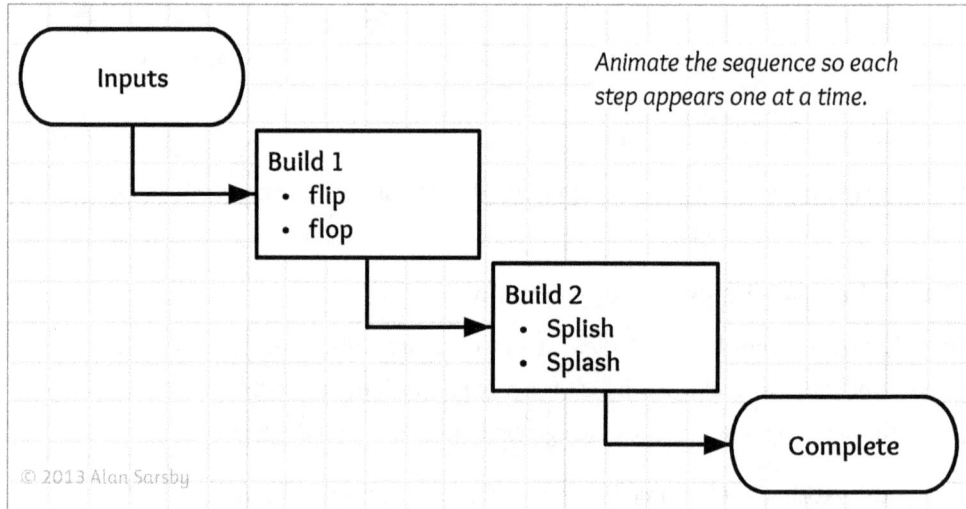

Figure 20: — A slow reveal reduces the audiences' cognitive load.

---

1   Learning styles are covered in the companion work A leader's guide to delivering training. The terminology, 'Theorist' is from the Honey and Mumford[2] model.
2   Honey, P. & Mumford, A. (1982) Manual of Learning Styles.

11 Slide content

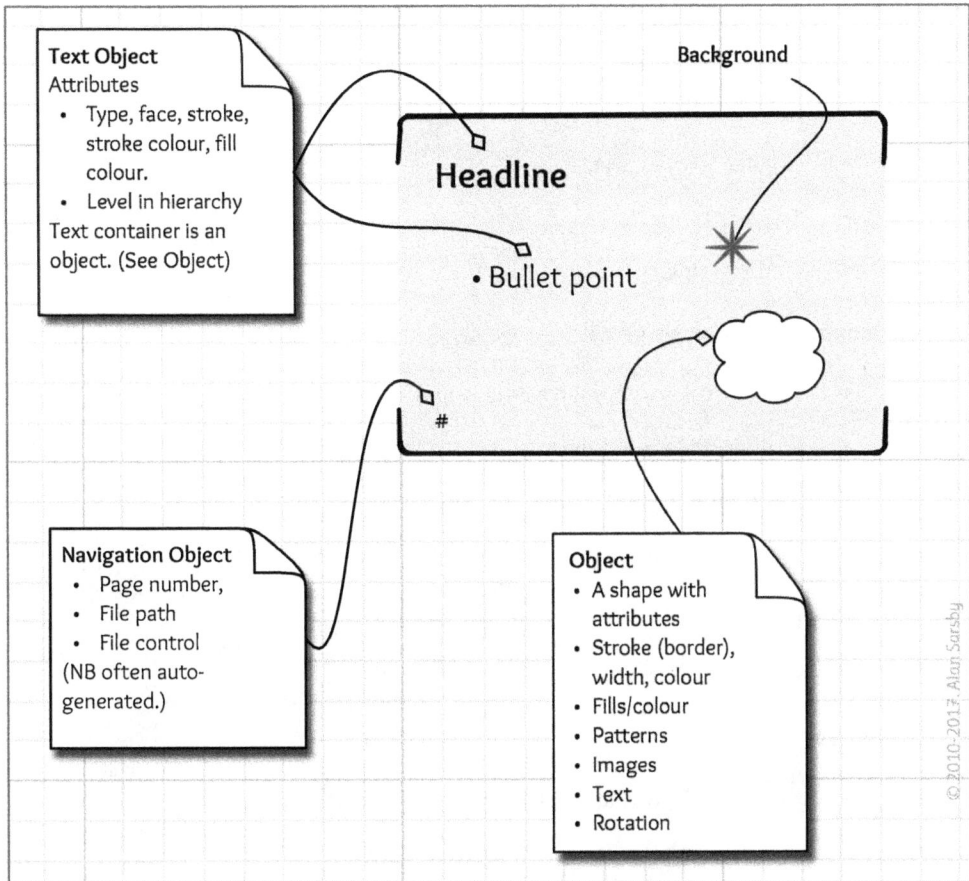

Figure 21: The Anatomy of a slide.

11.1   Ten forms of slide content

There are many things that could be drawn onto a slide; there might be an infinite number of choices. So to keep things simple this chapter concentrates on what might be the top ten.

Each of the following top-ten have their individual design requirements to make your presentation easier for you to deliver and easier for the audience to get the point.

1   **Charts and graphs**

    - Cartesian (x, y, z),
    - polar $A \angle \theta$ Graphs,
    - circular (pie) charts,
    - bar charts, and
    - scattergrams.

2   **Thinking and analysis grids**

    - Strategy grids 2x2, such as the popular SWOT.
    - Analysis grids, 3 x 3 grids.
    - Force-field, systems flows, and similar.

3   **Tables** (Rows and Columns).

    - Tabulations.
    - Spreadsheet data

4   **Images**

    - Photos to show real-world parts, details, and people.
    - Line drawings.

5   **Animations**

    - Moving elements
    - Video

6   **Diagrams**

    - Process diagrams, process control charts
    - Circuit diagrams
    - Schematics,
    - Maps.

7   **Infographics**

- A pictorial mixture of Graphs/Grids/Maps/Images

8   **Text**

- Lists and bullets

- Slogans and memorable phrases

- Labels

9   **Navigation** — The 'where are we' slide so your audience doesn't become lost.

10   **Summary** — The learning point or key message.

And additionally:

11   **Non-content elements**

- Headings, footers, slide numbers, and other non-content objects.

- Brand elements, logos, backgrounds

11.2   Charts and graphs

Spreadsheet and presentation software applications offer a vast range of charts and graphs! So how do you choose which one to use? It depends on what job you want it to do.

Two common forms of graphs are cartesian and polar.

Cartesian is the traditional x, y, z coordinates where some measurement or function relates the x-axis (the abscissa) to the y-axis (the ordinate). The relationship might be mathematical, such as a predictable $y = mx + c$, or observational such as experimental data, or tracking expenditure over time.

Polar graphs identify a point using a scalar (a magnitude) value extending from a reference point, and an angle from a reference direction.

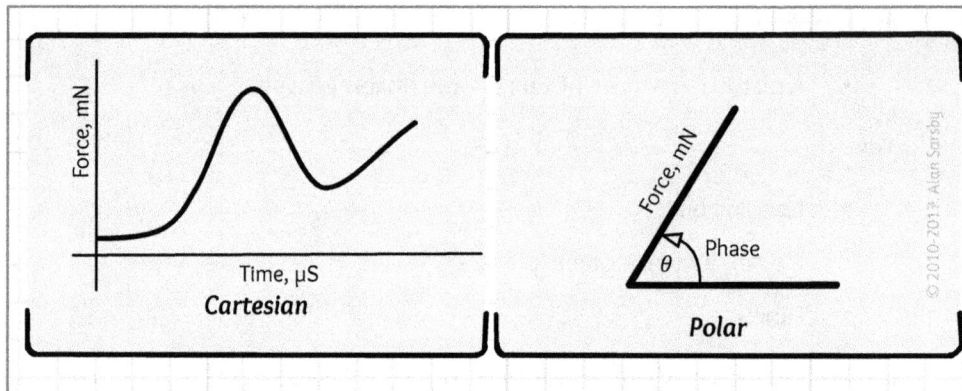

Figure 22: Cartesian and polar graphs.

For presentations, the 5s goal of Shine helps. Some suggestions:

- Remove the fine detail, these belong in a document. For a presentation, show the interpretation and draw the main curve in a thicker line so your audience can see the point you're making.

- Be economical with labels and notes — just enough so your audience can understand the point.

- Be honest — if you need to suppress the zero point to exaggerate small differences make it obvious on the graph, and say it aloud so you're not accused of cheating.

Pie charts — A popular variation of a polar graph is a pie-chart. The pie-chart is useful to show proportions and is generally easier to interpret than bar charts. Your software can generate a vast assortment of pie-charts — choose with clarity to the audience in mind.

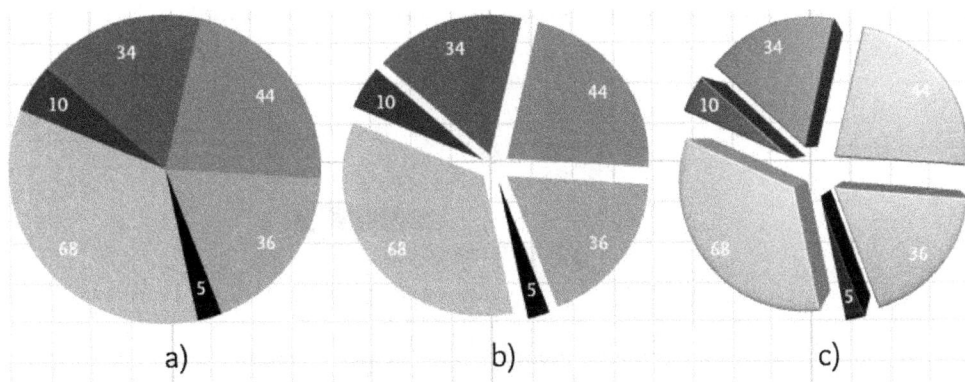

Figure 23: Pie charts (Cockscomb diagram[1]).

Exploded pie-charts are useful when you need de-clutter a fussy chart. An exploded chart separates the categories, or draws attention to a particular segment.

Note: see also 'segregation' and figure ground in § 9.3

---

1   A Cockscomb is the fleshy crest or protuberance on the head of a cockerel. The shape is usually in the form of a comb. Hence cockscomb. The Cockscomb diagram was famously used by Florence Nightingale to demonstrate that more solders died of infection than of battlefield injuries. (Crimean war, 1853–1856.) Some sources consider the polar cockscomb diagram to be the precursor of the pie chart. And hence Florence Nightingale is the inventor of pie charts.

By rotating and exploding the pie chart you can draw your audiences attention to specific detail. Figure 24 shows a rotated pie chart so the thinest segment stands out to the right. Its value '5' has been moved outside the segment.

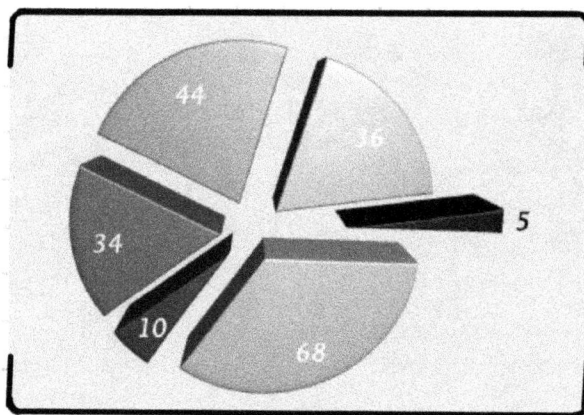

Figure 24: Pie chart with attention drawn to one segment.

By visually isolating one element (see segregation in §9.3), you draw your audiences' attention to the specific point you are making.

For example you can voice-over statements or questions, such as:

"How are we looking after these 5 customers?"

11.3 Strategy Grids

Strategy grids come in a variety of forms. Often in the form of 2 × 2, or n × n grids; others use zones to identify issues or potential actions. Figure 25, below, shows the popular SWOT[1] diagram.

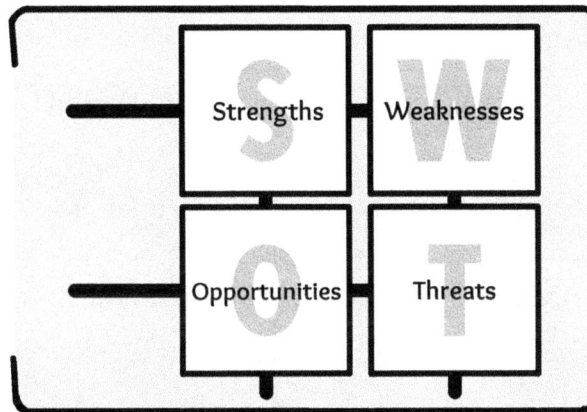

Figure 25: Example of a strategy grid – the SWOT analysis.

The fine details of the SWOT picture have been left out to make the basic diagram clear. The horizontal and vertical grid lines have been left in as a visual clue that there is more detail, but not on this diagram.

---

1   Note applying the advice to remove the fine details, this SWOT diagram is incomplete. For a treatment of SWOT, please see the companion volume A guide to swot for business studies students, Sarsby A, ISBN 978-0-9932504-2-2.

11.4   Tables

Tables are a mixed blessing in a projected image. Sometimes you need them to illustrate a choice or a point, and other-times they are just a visual fishing-net of incomprehensible numbers.

Some tactics for improving the projected quality of tables include:

- Only put up the row/column you need, and leave others out.

- Emphasise only the row/column with bold/colour and leave the others in a diminished state - faint or narrow texts, or faded colours.

- Design the table so that each row/column/total leads to a learning point that moves the story onwards.
  Avoid a tabulation of numbers that leads to a yawning so-what.

Examples:

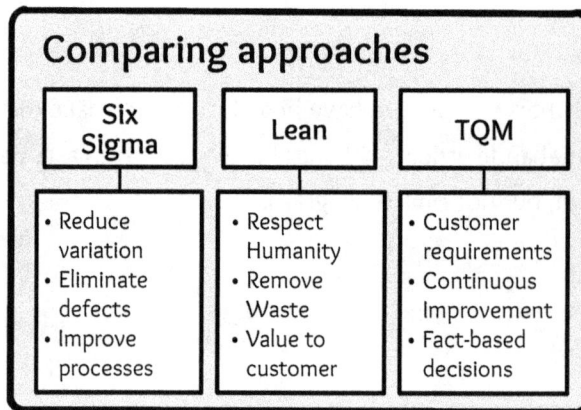

Figure 26: A simple form of tabulation.

This example is about the maximum that can be put on a slide.

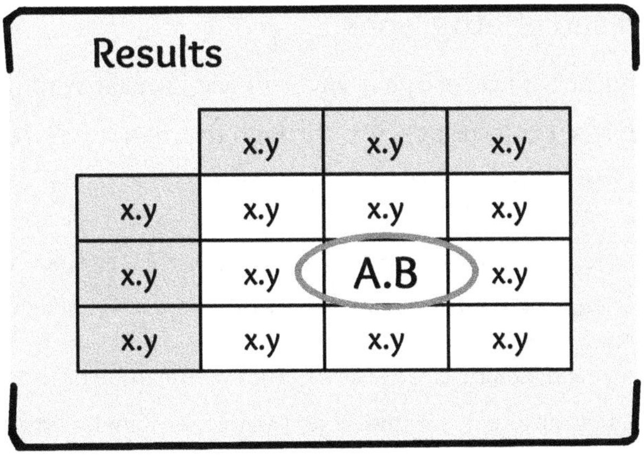

Figure 27: Isolate and exaggerate the key data point.

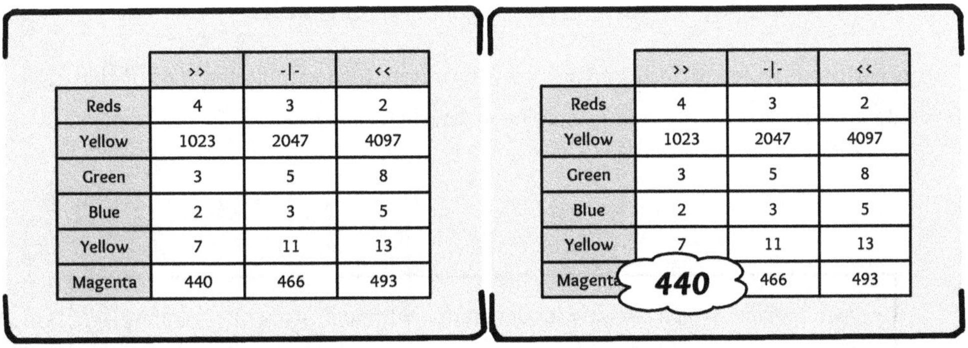

	>>	-|-	<<
Reds	4	3	2
Yellow	1023	2047	4097
Green	3	5	8
Blue	2	3	5
Yellow	7	11	13
Magenta	440	466	493

	>>	-|-	<<
Reds	4	3	2
Yellow	1023	2047	4097
Green	3	5	8
Blue	2	3	5
Yellow	7	11	13
Magenta	440	466	493

Figure 28: In dense tabulations, create a graphic to direct your audiences' attention.

The graphic can be overlaid as a click-to-reveal object so that the movement (the appearance) draws your audiences' attention to the important result in your table.

11.5   Images and photographs

Evolution comes to our aid once again. Humans are familiar with pictures, from earliest cave-paintings, Ecclesiastical art, through to a variety of modern forms. For business presentations, the two major forms are:

Records — images that are factual record of an object or place. These can range from a photo of a science-like object, a laboratory picture, or records of scenes.

Pictorial — images which include beauty as a goal. These can be both factual, for example, a landscape, or a created object you have manufactured.

Design guides for the use of images and photography include:

Relevance — the image must be relevant to your topic and purpose. It is even better if the image is taken by, or of, you depicting your contribution.

Composition — review the image for its composition, for example the rule-of-thirds, lead-in lines, and importantly a point of interest.

Avoid images which are only for decoration. Although stock photography agencies can provide high-quality images, take care that these are suitable and relevant. Some specific images are now so common-place they have become cliché. Others, especially in customer service situations have become known by a derogatory phrase (very politically incorrect) and your audience might groan when seeing them.

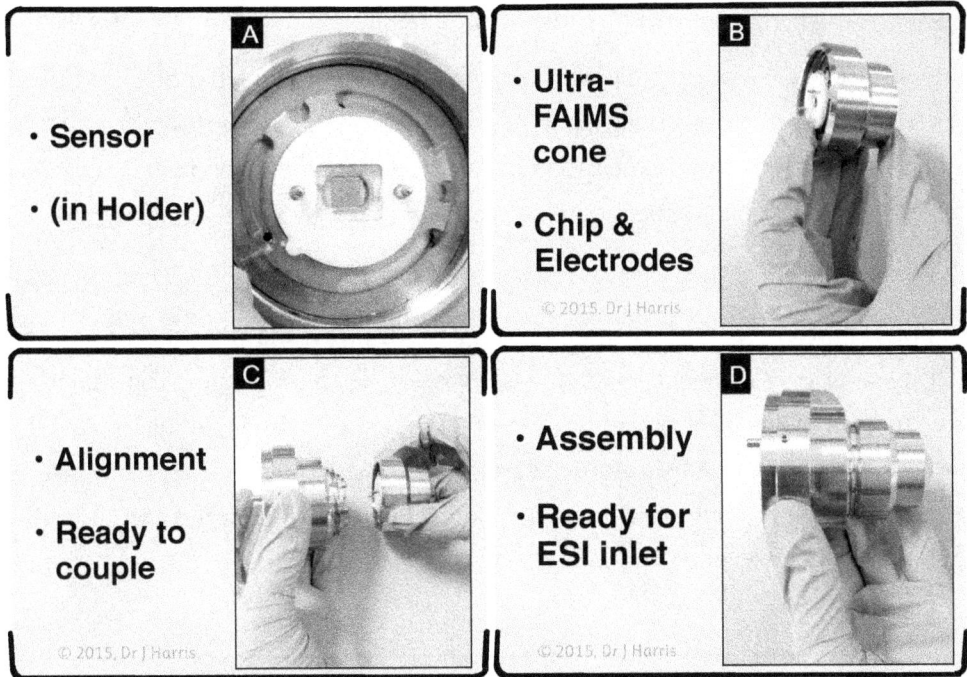

Figure 29: A sequence of slides to show an assembly.

Note: The audience for this sequence were scientists familiar with Mass-Spectrometry, which means:

- The photographs are relevant.
- The abbreviations FAIMS and ESI are familiar working jargon to the audience.

The operator's hand gives a sense of scale to the assembly.

The consistency of slide design, summary text on left, photograph on right, conveys a sense of coherence to the sequence.

FAIMS, Field Asymmetric waveform Ion Mobility Spectrometry.
ESI, Electrospray Ionisation.

11.6   Animations and videos

Showing videos in a presentation has benefits and hazards. One the one hand they can be useful for demonstrating subjects which are not easily be described. On the other hand a video changes the mood of the presentation environment. Your audience can switch into 'lounge-mode', relaxing as if they were watching the television at home.

To prevent the audience dipping into 'lounge-mode', treat the video viewing as an activity. Brief your audience to do things, for example to take notes. You can be even more specific: brief one group to take notes on the man in the blue suit, another to follow the lady in a green cardigan, and so on. You can normally give several different briefings to a group so that everyone stays engaged and knows their part in the debriefing and review.

> Author's tip: Try to keep the room lit whilst showing a video. Dimming the lights is a subtle clue for your audience to drop out of 'listen and learn' mode and into 'lounge-mode.'
>
> If you have to turn the lights off for visibility, try to turn off only those lights nearest the screen, and leave others switched on.

Commercially purchased videos have advantages and disadvantages. The main advantage is that professional actors deliver a slick performance, displaying a realistic situation to support a point. However, even apparently generic subjects are unlikely to use the same underlying model that you want to transfer to your audience; you'll need to be selective in which parts you show.

If you are making your own video — there is a need for additional skills. These include scripting, (based on a story arc for the video). camera operations, sound capture, set and production, and post-production editing.

Preparation

If you've decided that a video is the way to go, then:

- Test everything beforehand. VHS (*) and DVD players are mechanical contraptions with a propensity to fail when it is most urgent.

- Remember that VHS and DVD mechanisms are slow to react to signals from the remote or front panel controls.

- If you can, show videos from your computer and make each element a separate file which you can embed into the presentation. (See also Appendix 5.)

- Set up the exact start and finish points, so that you don't show unnecessary parts of the video.

(*) VHS is an obsolete technology, however some (especially training and historical) videos tend to be expensive, so the business case for a like-for-like replacement of a worn-out VHS tape for a new DVD is often difficult to make.

Some very specialist subjects survive only on old VHS tape. You should assume that some old VHS tapes are still current.

Even DVDs are becoming obsolete, and some modern portable computers are no longer equipped with an optical drive for CDs and DVDs.

11.7 Infographics

Infographics are diagrams that represent data and information using a pictorial approach often mixing several techniques. Infographics tend to be a collection of metaphors, as such they need careful design and careful consideration to be sure your audience understands the point.

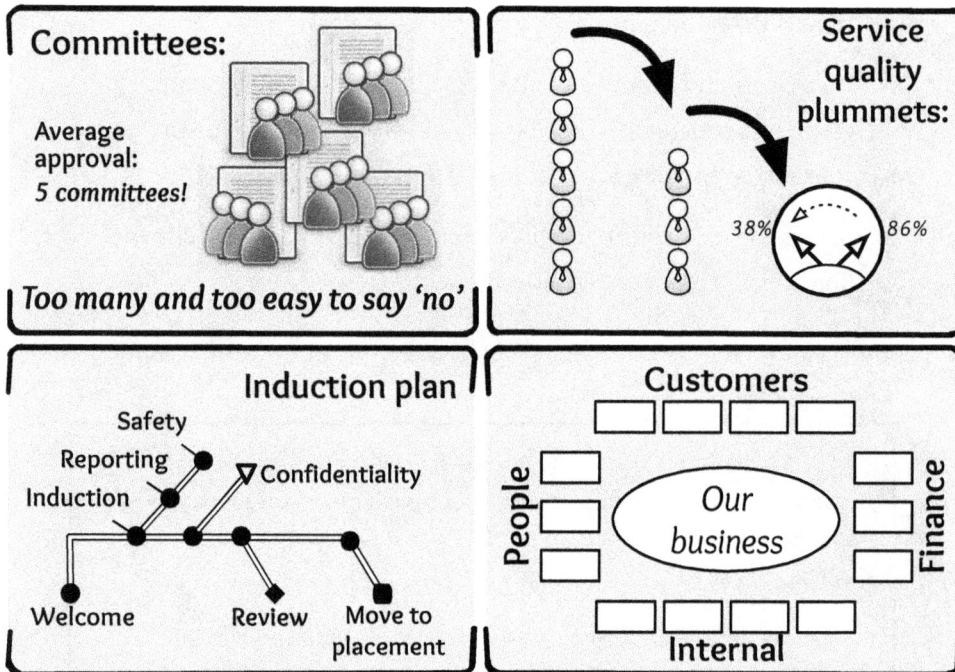

Figure 30: Examples of infographic slides.

Design guides for infographics include:

- **Size** — Infographics can become large illustrations. Test that your infographic fits in the limited space of a slide. Otherwise, consider reducing the content and supply a supporting handout, or use a large-format wall chart.

- **Voice-over** — Infographics are inherently fussy and complex. They benefit from restricting the number of graphic elements, and making more use of your voiceover.
  The service quality example (Figure 30) a voiceover could be something like:
  "In two years, our service team has reduced from 50 skilled technicians to 30. In the same period, our customer satisfaction ratings have plummeted from 86% to an embarrassingly poor 38%. We should revisit those two-year old decisions."

- **Slow reveal** — Because infographics contain many elements, your audience gain a better understanding if the key points are revealed one-at-a-time. For example:

  - *"Committees! Our company is littered with them. [Click - Reveal graphics icons]*

  - *Did you know to gain approval for a project, it takes, on average, a proposal to go through five committees, yes five!*
    [Click - Reveal text 'Average ... 5 committees']

  - *The conclusion is easy to see*
    [Click - to reveal the next text 'Too many ...']

  - *We have too many committees.*

  - *... and it is too easy for each committee to say 'no' and block the progress."*

With many elements on an infographic, the audience are free to work their way though it in any order they choose. Invest some energy in working out an effective way to guide your audience through the complexity. Slow reveals and clear voiceovers are essential.

Other design approaches include

- Day in the life of, and other journey-based formats, including the classic *'staple yourself to ...'*

- Jigsaws. (But take care — as a visual metaphor it is overused, and strongly associated with a specific software company.)

- Transport-style maps.

- Scorecards.

11.8   Diagrams

Diagrams come in many forms: A process diagram, a system forces diagram, a topological diagram, and many others.

The approach for what might be complex diagrams is to keep them simple with only the relevant details. In the circuit diagram of Figure 31, only the essential details are shown — it shows the principle of an operational amplifier using negative feedback. Details such as the power supply, noise suppression, and the virtual earth are all omitted.

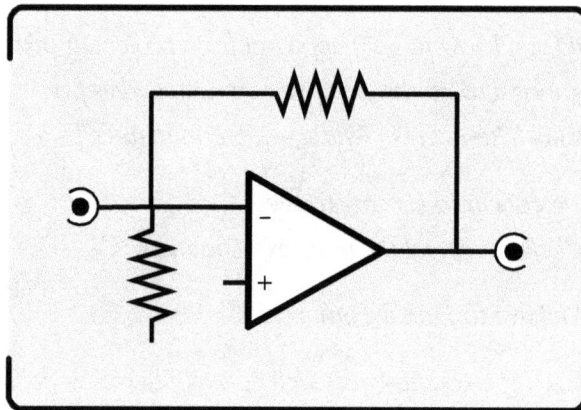

Figure 31: Keep it simple — show principles, not every detail.

From the 5S approach:
Sort — *Keep only the necessary items in the workplace.*
When applied to presentations becomes:
Put only the necessary items on a slide.

11.9 Text and lists

11.9.1 Yes, text!

Despite the oft-seen advice of not putting text or bullet points on a slide, sometimes you need to. If your subject matter requires text, then pay attention to:

11.9.2 Typography

Typography is the craft of arranging type (fonts) the letters, numbers, symbols, and other glyphs in a manner to meet some purpose.

Terminology

A typeface is the shape and form of the numbers and letters. For example Helvetica is a typeface. The Regular, Italic and Bold versions of Helvetica are separate 'faces'. Thus *Helvetica Bold is a typeface*.

A font is a Typeface rendered at specific size. Hence, *Helvetica Regular 10 point* is a font.

By convention, the normal face for a san serif face is known as Regular; for a serif face it is known as Roman.

The distinction between a face and a font has become blurred. The use of 'font' is often used to refer to both the face (typeface) and its size (font) is technically incorrect. (Despite some software's use of 'font' in their menus.)

Legibility

Legibility is made up of many factors, including:

- The height of lower-case letters compared to the height of the upper-case letters. This is known as the x-height. There is no standard ratio for the x-height; it is whatever the designer of the typeface chooses. You have no control over the x-height; it is built into the typeface by its designer.

- The length (number of words and characters) in a line. Newspaper columns are narrow, typically fitting about five words per row. This enables the reader to scan each line in a single sweep. The classical book design[1] (novels) is between 50 − 70 characters per line. This length enables the reader to scan the line in three-to-five hops.

- The spacing between lines. The distance between the baseline and the next (or previous) line is the 'point size' of the font. You can add space (technically known as *leading — rhymes with spreading*) between the lines to make it easier to read.

> In this book, the type is set at 12/17 (spoken as 12 on 17 point). This fraction in typography means 12 point text with a 17 point leading.

Point size

Although the 'point' unit might be standard (in Adobe Postscript, a point is exactly $^1/_{72}$ of an inch). The size of the characters are not. Figure 32 shows a selection of typefaces (font) — Georgia 24pt is used as a reference, and compared to other common faces which have been adjusted (font size) to make them, optically, the same size.

The point of this point[2] is not to become hung-up with rigidly following a rule about using, say, 28pt text. The important aim is to make the text optically large enough to be read by the audience at the back of the room.

---

1 This book is not of classical design.
2 Sorry about the pun.

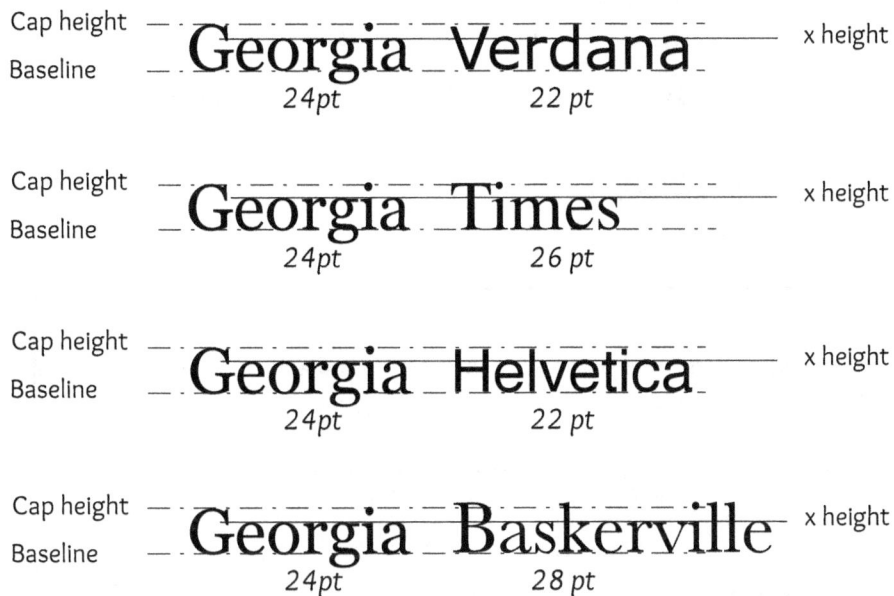

Cap height		x height
Baseline	Georgia Verdana	
	24pt 22 pt	

Cap height		x height
Baseline	Georgia Times	
	24pt 26 pt	

Cap height		x height
Baseline	Georgia Helvetica	
	24pt 22 pt	

Cap height		x height
Baseline	Georgia Baskerville	
	24pt 28 pt	

Figure 32: Identical optical sizes range from 22–28 points!

In keeping with the earlier advice to show only the essential details, Figure 32 only shows the minimum construction lines to make the point about point sizes. In typographic design, there are additional construction lines not shown in Figure 32.

All capitals

Text all in capitals is difficult to read because a competent reader looks at whole words at once, not individual letters.

The left-hand outline in Figure 33 is readily interpreted as the word 'quality'. The word on the right could be QUIETLY, QUACKED, or QUADPLEX. The rectangular shape of the outline removes the reading clues.

Figure 33: The outline shape of a word aids reading.

TEXT ALL IN CAPITALS AND BOLD MAKES READING MORE DIFFICULT.

Avoid words in all-capitals unless you have a very specific reason to use them.

Respect for humanity:
Some dyslexics find text in all-capitals almost impossible to read.
And this author is dyslexic ...

Serif and san-serifs

In Figure 34, the left-hand letter E is displayed in Gill Sans, this is 'san-serif' (without serif) typeface. The serifs are the small ornaments at the end of each stroke. The right-hand letter E is in Times, which is a serif typeface.

Both are set in 48pt and scaled to show the difference when projected to a large screen. The Times font renders the serifs as a staircase pattern to give the optical illusion of a smooth curve. The effect works well on a monitor or on paper. But, the projector screen is a scaled-up copy of the monitor, so the staircase pattern of the serifs become easily visible. This rendering of the serifs is what makes the font scruffy. And in turn this scruffiness is a distraction, which is a visual waste. Eliminate the waste.

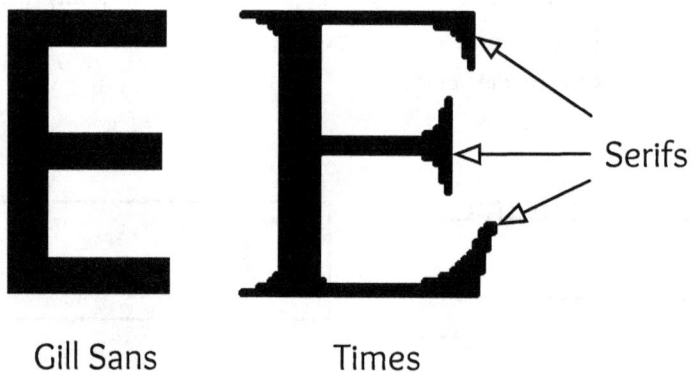

Gill Sans   Times

Serifs

Figure 34: Contrasting serif and san-serif fonts.

> *From six-sigma, the 5S approach:*
> *Shine — Clean the work so it is neat and tidy. (Not scruffy.)*

Choose a robust san serif typeface (font); these show well through low-resolution projectors. San serif fonts include: Helvetica, Arial, Cambria, and Gill Sans. Serif fonts, such as Times New Roman, can lose their detail and become 'scruffy' on screen.

11.9.3 Bullet points

Bullet points are a mainstay feature of presentations. They are much derided and are an overused feature strongly associated with a poor presentation. However sometimes bullet points are the right tool for your purpose and your audience; if that is the case, and you must use bullets then some useful design approaches are:

Coherence: One concept per list

Bullet points are inherently lists. Each point should should be related. For example, the left-column is a list of white wine grape varieties. The right-column is the same list with some other topics interspersed.

Table 3: Coherence in lists.

Coherent list	Incoherent list
• Bosco Bianco	• Bosco Bianco
• Chardonnay	• Chardonnay
• Chenin blanc	• Course work
• Colombard	• Colombard
• Riesling	• Street crime
• Sauvignon	• Riesling
• Viognier	• Worms

In the coherent list, your audience can guess that Bosco Bianco is a grape variety because the other members of the list are grape varieties. They can further guess it is a white grape because the others are white-wine varieties.

In the incoherent list, the absence of subject coherence means that Bosco Bianco could be the name of a spanner, or indeed, anything!

You risk confusing your audience with incoherent lists. Confusing the audience is a disengagement which invites them to do something else; use their smartphones, read other papers, and so on.

Action lists or descriptive lists

Action lists are those where each bullet point starts with a verb. These are useful if your object is to encourage your audience to perform some activity.

Descriptive lists are those where each bullet is a description and mostly start with a noun. These are useful where your objective is to transfer small chunks of knowledge.

Mixing action and description in the same list disorients your audience. Disorientation leads to confusion, and hence to disengagement.

Table 4: Comparing lists with leading verbs, with leading nouns..

Action list with leading verbs	Descriptive lists with leading nouns

• Organise the team launch. • Complete the pre-event checklist. • Book a venue.	• The project takes 6 months. • A narrow and precise scope. • The team is self-selected.

Minimise bullet *content*

Sometimes, bullet points have their place. A bullet point is be a few key words to make a point. A presentation slide multiple bullets of full sentences is a crib sheet for you; don't show it to your audience, it has no value for them.

Minimise the *length* of the bullet list

Organise your list so that it comprises a small number list items per list (for example, 4, no greater than 7). This makes it easier for your audience to digest the list as a single entity.

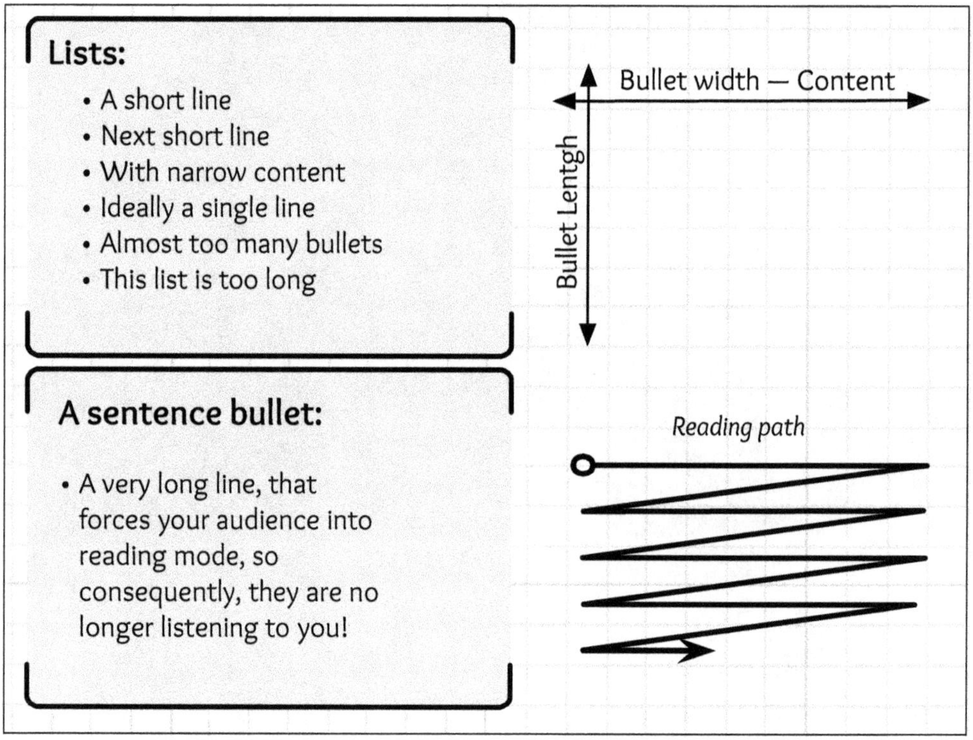

Figure 35: Bullet points — content, length, and reading.

11.9.4 Text on slides

Figure 36 is a great example of how **not** to use text in a presentation. The example is (possibly) lifted from a report; the language is dense, imprecise, and bureaucratic.

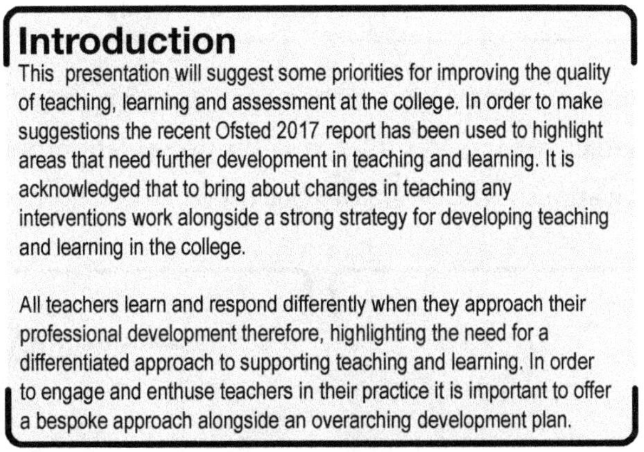

Introduction

This presentation will suggest some priorities for improving the quality of teaching, learning and assessment at the college. In order to make suggestions the recent Ofsted 2017 report has been used to highlight areas that need further development in teaching and learning. It is acknowledged that to bring about changes in teaching any interventions work alongside a strong strategy for developing teaching and learning in the college.

All teachers learn and respond differently when they approach their professional development therefore, highlighting the need for a differentiated approach to supporting teaching and learning. In order to engage and enthuse teachers in their practice it is important to offer a bespoke approach alongside an overarching development plan.

Figure 36: Phew!

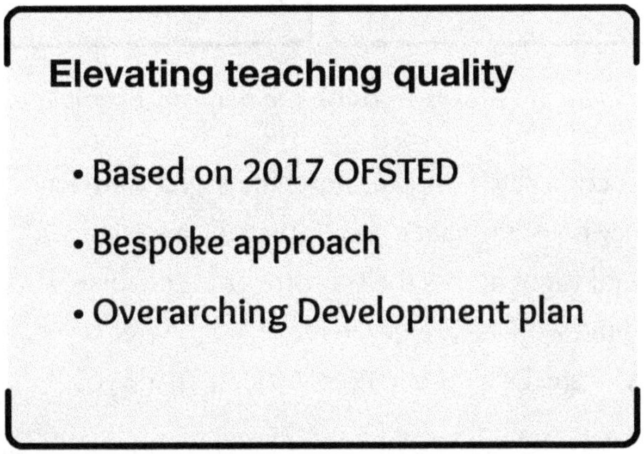

Elevating teaching quality

- Based on 2017 OFSTED

- Bespoke approach

- Overarching Development plan

Figure 37: Audience-friendly version — short and to the point!

11.10 Brand elements

If you work for a corporate-like organisation, it is likely there is a company style guide or brand guide. Make use of it as you can and adapt it for your audience.

> The original notion of 'brand' was a mark scorched into an animal's hind to depict ownership of the animal. The modern equivalent is a combination of logo, colour scheme, and typeface (font).

A modern interpretation is more comprehensive: A brand is the *whole experience* your customer (audience) acquires from you, the presentation, and the points your are making. And vicariously, the brand of your organisation/company.

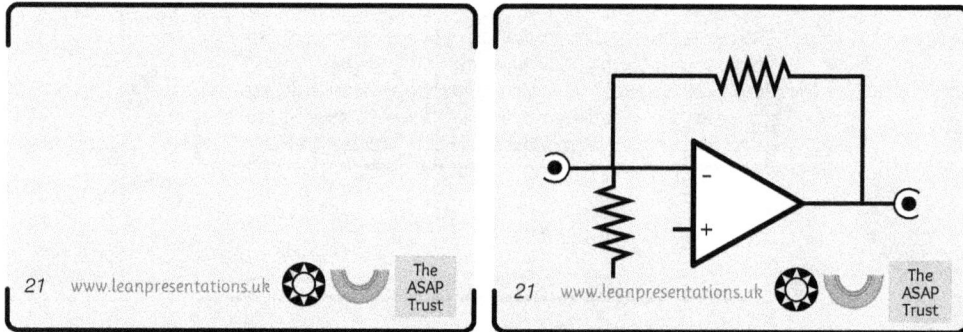

Figure 38: Excess logos on the corporate template.

On the (fictitious) corporate template (left) the logos seem innocent enough on a blank slide; but they consume space and potentially interfere with the slide content. A parade of logos across the bottom, or even worse, also down the right-hand side reduces the working area even more. Logo litter is very distracting. It is visual noise, it is a waste. Don't use it. Press Delete. Thank you.

Restrict yourself to logos only on the opening and closing slides. This leaves the intermediate story slides to take advantage of the available space and avoids the distracting logo litter.

11.11 Navigation — where are we?

If your presentation covers multiple topics, or major subsections, a navigation slide helps your audience to know where they are. Such a slide is helpful in the introductory elements, then later to define the end of a subsection.

Navigation slides are useful. For example to explain that pre-knowledge is needed before the main event of your presentation. This conveys a value to the prerequisite parts of your presentation that some audience members might otherwise ignore and disengage.

As an example: Near the beginning of your presentation, deliver the navigation slide as a slow reveal:

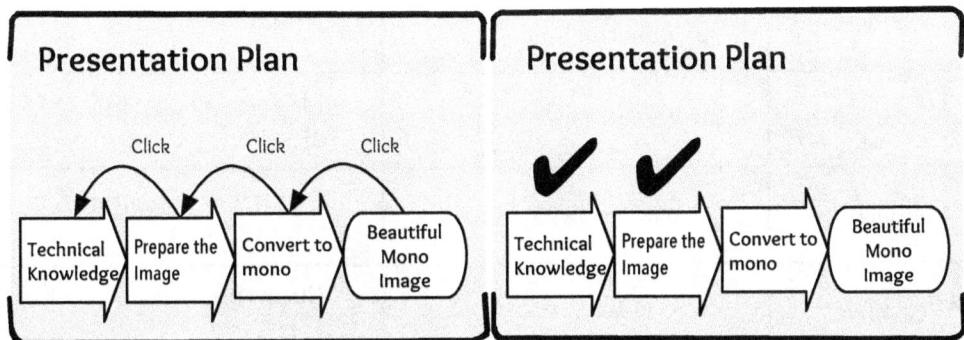

Figure 39: A navigation slide (left), then later (right) to reward progress.

- Begin with the objective *(A Beautiful Mono Image)* then work backwards with successive reveals, to show the sequence of the story-arc is going to take so that the audience knows what's coming. And why they need to invest in the pre-knowledge.

- Announce where you are starting; in the example the *Technical Knowledge* is first; present that section, and at the end of that subsection, announce it is finished accompanied by a closing visual. Likewise, at the end of the second subsection *(Preparing the image)* the progress visual would look like the right-hand example of Figure 39.

    There is important psychology at work here: The end-of-subsection rewards your audience with a progress indicator (more engagement) and a sense of accomplishment.

11.12 Slide headings

Headings announce to your audience what the slide is about. There are broadly seven types of headings:

Table 5: Forms of slide headings.

	Heading format	Example
A Question	A short sentence, or keywords as questions	Why draw a diagram?
A Statement	Truncated sentences with at least a noun and a verb	Guide your viewer
A Phrase/Topic	Short phrase - predominately nouns	Helpful tips for …
A Headline	Newspaper style headline.	Man bites dog (What, again!)
A listicle	Number + statement	7 drivers of customer dissatisfaction
Weird Trick	An odd statement	Clean your toilet with cola (*)
How to	'How to' + topic	How to change your font colour.

(*) This weird trick does actually work. Cola contains Phosphoric acid (H_3O_4P) a non-toxic acid (thank goodness for that) which is an effective reagent, a bleach.
A 2 litre bottle of cola is usually less expensive than a 250 ml of bleach. And much less of a worry if you spill some on the floor.

Questions are useful because they engage your viewer by teasing them to answer the question, or to raise their expectation that you are going to answer the question. Questions can be those that your audience already knows the answer to, or those they don't know the answer to, or questions that the audience didn't think of (insights) *"Ohh, I didn't think of that ..."*

See also, Engagement in §6

However, a long presentation using only questions places a cognitive demand on your audience; for every slide, the audience tries to answer the question. The prolonged cognitive effort might be mentally exhausting and result in disengagement. An effective approach is to start a theme with a question, and then to use other forms of headings for intermediate elements of the story.

For some audiences, the classic so-called left brainers, topic headings are a good match because that's how they expect to receive information. Take care because abbreviated text can often be read in different ways, be vague, or is simply noise (and hence a waste).

11.13 Slide footers

It is possible to include a great deal of distracting objects in the slide footer. (Look again at Figure 38.) However there are two objects that deserve a place in the slide footer. One for you, and one for the audience.

Slide number

Way back in the 1970s and 80s, slides were printed onto transparent acetate sheets. Back then, a presenter's biggest fear was not the audience, nor the material, but the ever-present danger that the acetates would fall onto the floor[1]. Apart from the embarrassment if this happened during the presentation, was the task of reassembling the sheets in the right order. A slide number (like a page number) made this job a lot easier.

---

1 Acetates were apt to become electrostatically charged, then as if by magic, jumped onto the floor! In addition to landing in a random order, they attracted dust, muck, and other debris, so it took additional time to clean them ready for projection. And in the meantime, the audience were disengaging.

Your audience also benefits from slide numbers: You can ask (engage them) that if they would like to return to a particular slide it would be helpful to keep a note of the slide number. Your projection software has easy ways to go directly to a slide during the presentation.

File tracer

A file tracer is a reference to where the file is located on your computer.
This helps you locate the file (possibly months or years) after the presentation. File tracers help you with audit and retrieval.

```
C:\Documents\Projects\Sapphire\Project_awareness\Stakholders.ppt
~/"Lean Presentations"/"LG 2 Lean Presentations" LPv-216.key
```

The tracer is only read by you, possibly only on paper. Format the tracer in a small typeface and font size so it doesn't distract your audience.

Use a file tracer only on the title slide, otherwise it contributes to the logo litter and restricts the working space in the slides.

12 Handouts

Table 6: A handout Is/Is Not analysis

	Handout Is	Handout Is Not	Therefore (Design input)	Therefore (Value for customer)
Why	Supports topic with a purpose and objectives	Is not an ego trip.	Supports a point/goal.	I understand it.
What	A gift. A (small) document.	Is not a copy of the slides.	What point is to explained further.	Easy to recollect.
When	After the presentation.	Not an interruption	Referenced at the right point in the story.	Relevant and not a distraction.
Where	A follow up, in an email, or in the foyer.	Not embedded in the presentation	Standalone document.	Audience stay within the story.
Who	You! Your words and pictures.	A handout is not a substitute for you.	Speaks with the presenter's voice.	Frees your audience to follow your story.
How	Designed as a handout.	Slide miniatures from the software.	Visual consistency.	Align with the brand values of the presenter.

12.1   The purpose of a handout

The purpose of any handout is to help the audience absorb and learn the subject. Handouts carry knowledge, information, procedures, guidelines ... *and your reputation*. If you need handouts, It is worth designing and producing good handouts.

Handouts support several functions, including:

- The take-home gift.

- The how-to-contact-me, much like a business card.

- Reference material for use in the workplace.

- It frees the audience from the tyranny of the mechanical 'hear-copy-write process', so they can engage in cognitive activities such as analysis or sense-making.

- It releases you from the burden of putting too much detail on the slides.

If you can't find a purpose for handouts, don't use them just for the sake of it. Reapply the principles of Figure 13 (page 44) to handouts — so that you know whether to invest in the creation of a handout. Alternatively use a variation of the presentation charter §4.3 to create a handout charter (see Figure 8).

> Note: it is always worth having a separate handouts for your use as the speaker. Your version might include the answers to a quiz, points to bring out, notes, and other helpful jottings. You could print these on coloured paper so they are easily distinguishable from those you give to the audience.

12.2   Design principles for handouts

The design principles for handouts are, unsurprisingly, the same as those for designing slides. The difference is in the context.

Context

- A single slide doesn't stand by itself. A slide depends on the previous slides and sets up the audience for the next slide.
  By comparison, a handout is a self-contained document.

- A slide is part of the presentation delivery.
  A handout is taken away and read later when convenient to the audience.

- A slide is a pictorial communication projected onto a screen. A handout is a mixed text/diagrammatic document printed onto paper.

Handouts deserve the same care and attention you give to the creation of your whole presentation and the accompanying slides. Unsurprisingly, the design principles for creating handouts are identical to the design principles introduced earlier.

Design principle 1 — Purpose. The handout must have a purpose. Without a purpose the handout is a waste — don't even write it!

Design principle 2 — Fit to the audience. Adapt the content to match your audience. For example the vocabulary and jargon, building on what they already know. Hence, you must understand your audience.

Design principle 3 — Content to noise ratio. The content is the message, idea, or purpose; noise is anything that is not relevant or distracts from that purpose.

Design principle 4 — Story arch for handouts. Your whole presentation is supported by a story arc, see §5.3, and the example in Figure 10.
A handout needs its own story arc.

Design principle 5 — Effective redundancy. The content of the handout is a different way of expressing the same (but extra) content given in the presentation with words and visuals. This handout reinforces the effective redundancy.

Design principle 6 — Coherent and consistent. If your handout is incoherent your audience becomes lost, especially if reading it some time after the presentation; if they are inconsistent there is a risk that your audience might think they're reading a handout from a different presentation.

12.3   Designing a handout

The need for handouts follow the same principles for the presentation:

Why

Handouts need a reason to exist and justify your time in creating them. Reasons might include:

- To give background information, which if included in the main presentation would be a distraction (a waste).

- To give detail that is beyond what can fit on a slide.

- To give supplementary details, such as resources, web addresses, and so on.

- To be your 'business card' — your contact details, phone, email, webpage.

Purpose

The handouts need an purpose. Examples might be:

- To demonstrate a principle — for example, a derivation, a model, or a need.

- To show a 'how to' — to show how something is achieved. For example, how a red widget fits into the green thingy.

- To summarise the message.

The same tests from §4.1 can be applied to handouts:

"The purpose of this handout is to ...   ."

Story arc and style

Handouts are a self-contained small documents. To make them flow, handouts also need a story arc.

The style of how the handout speaks to its viewer varies from formal to light. It could be an abstract, or a newsletter/magazine style article. The choice is yours.

Author's note: A handout starts as being your pictures/content/words, but as soon as the audience writes upon it, the handout becomes their property - not yours. They have taken ownership of it.

If you can, encourage your audience to make notes/doodles/pictures on their copy of the handout — which means you should build a deliberate time gap for your audience to make their notes.

12.4 Handouts that are not handouts

Copies of slides

Modern presentation software has functions to create so-called handouts. Except that they are not handouts, they are copies of the slides. It is lazy and not audience friendly.

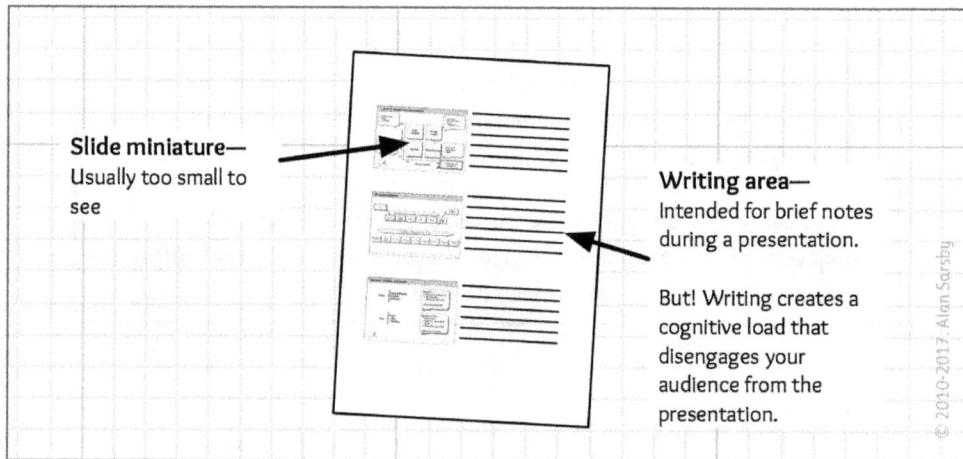

Figure 40: Example of an unsuitable handout.

Copies of the notes

A slightly less poor approach is to use the software's Notes pages.

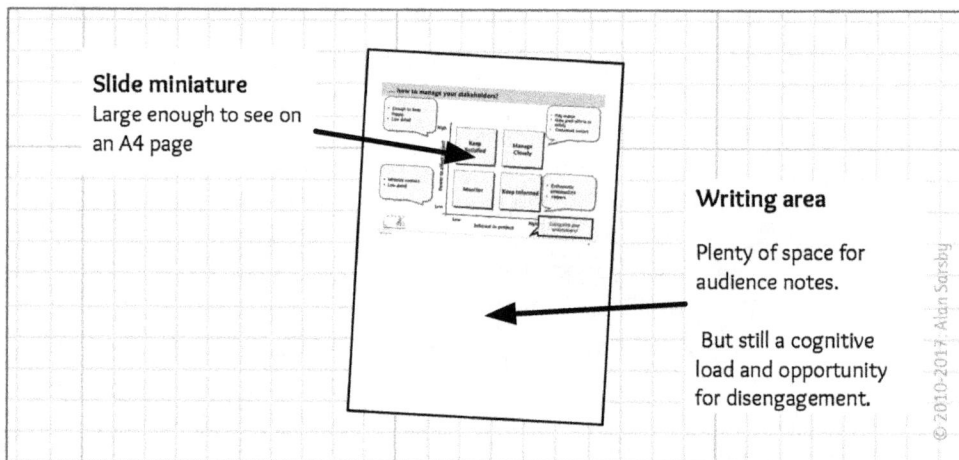

Figure 41: Using the Notes pages; it is a copy of the slides, not a handout.

However, both Figure 40 and Figure 41 are examples of printing the slides and calling them handouts. Figure 41 *might* have a use in a training session where the tutor (presenter) can halt the flow and create note-taking time for the participants.

> Note: To edit the notes page, head to PowerPoint's View menu, then Master>Notes master. (It depends on your version of PowerPoint, but the help function should point you in the right direction). In Apple Keynote a similar function is in the print dialog.

Copies of reports or dissertations

Reports and dissertations can be huge documents. They have a structure and purpose which is very likely to be different from your presentation's story arc. These are definitely not handouts.

13 Your words

13.1   Words — use and abuse

The spoken word is easy to misuse. And sometimes, deviously, by poor quality speakers who try to make themselves sound better than they are!

In crafting the spoken part of your presentation, it is worth paying attention to:

Business clichés — also known as 'consultant-speak' and 'management-speak'. These litter our business communications. For example, thinking outside the box, paradigm shift, and take it to the next level. Often, these phrases sound evangelical and convincing; in reality they are empty, ambiguous, and actionless.

Metaphors— We use metaphors in everyday language. For example: *as useless as a chocolate teapot*. Clearly, a chocolate teapot would melt when boiling water is poured in. Except that even this simple metaphor doesn't work where the culture is to drink iced tea, even a chocolate teapot might have a use!
There are thousands of these metaphors — they add variety and colour to casual messages.

The main danger is that the metaphor is not understood by your audience, especially if English is not their native language.

Auxiliary verbs — need extra words. Auxiliary verbs need a main verb to work with, this has two side effects: it increases the number of words you have to speak; and it can make you sound bureaucratic. Some examples ...

- *...will contain*, is clearer when simplified to *contains*

- *The volume will be increased* is simpler as *The volume is increased*, or even simpler to ... *increases the volume*.

Double negatives — Double negatives increase the words you need to speak, reduce the clarity of what you are saying, and place a cognitive load on your listener as they decode what (they think) you meant.

The interpretation of a double negative depends on the reader's version of English. Is it two negatives cancelling each other to leave a positive; alternatively, is it a reinforcement of the negative. Your audience makes the choice, not you!

- *It's not unusual* — a subtle way of saying it is common.

- *I don't know nothing* — Estuary English for I don't know anything.

> Note — Estuary English is a dialect associated with the East of London and the Thames estuary. The BBC television series EastEnders made some of the dialect more common nationally. Some of the East-End dialect is only intelligible to people in the immediate locality of the East End.

Idioms — An idiom is a phrase or sentence that means something other than the sum of its words. Idioms can be common, known to many people, or exclusive to a particular group or community. Idioms can be risky in presentations because your audience might not know how to infer the meaning; especially if the idiom has a regional basis. For example in US English *'an end run'* is a phrase borrowed from US football meaning a tactical manoeuvre to evade the defenders. In UK English, few people know the rules and styles of play in US football, and consequently the idiom is meaningless.

If you can, avoid idioms, and explain what you mean.

Sarcasm — For some people sarcasm is a normal mode of communicating. They find fault with everything and are generally negative. Using sarcasm in your presentation puts your reputation is at risk.

Internet speak — Internet speak (netspeak/cyber-slang) had a purpose in the early days of email to save space and transmission time. It is still common in text messages. However, speaking netspeak aloud in your presentation runs the risk of your audience forming an opinion that you are a sarcastic, self-centred, individual. And oops — there goes your reputation.

An example

> The proposal IMNSHO and NAGI.
>
> Spoken as The proposal is *imn-sho* and *nag-i*.
>
> Translation: *In my not so humble opinion and not a good idea.*

Jargon — Jargon saves time, but adds exclusivity. Using jargon might be frowned upon, but in some cases your subject matter and audience might expect it of you. For an audience knowledgable in six-sigma, they would expect you to speak the abbreviations DMAIC or 5S without elaboration, for web designers they would expect you to say HTML, DOM, and CSS without further explanation.

The golden rule for jargon is to use it iff[1] your audience are already fluent it it, and it suits the subject matter.

Use shorter words — Most long words are polysyllabic and can be difficult, especially those with English as foreign language, to pronounce or to de-code. Most long words have a shorter equivalent. Use the shorter word.

Negative phrases — A negative phrase conveys what you want to restrict but leaves open what you'd like to achieve. Positive phrasing often requires fewer words. See Table 7 for some examples.

Table 7: Comparison of negative and positive expressions.

Negative phrase	Equivalent positive phrase
Does not include	Leaves out
Not often	Rarely
Don't forget to ...	Remember to ...

1The term 'iff' is not a misspelling. It is mathematical jargon meaning 'if, and *only* if.

Passive voice — increases words and reduces responsibility

Using the active voice for your message has a huge impact on clarity of your message. The active voice usually needs fewer words than the passive voice, and it adds clarity by associating the doer with the action. For example:

Table 8: Comparing passive and active voice..

Passive voice	Active voice
The ball was thrown by John.	John threw the ball.
A frog was kissed by a princesses.	The princess kissed the frog.
The application must be completed by the student and received by the bursar's office by 1 June. [17 words]	The bursar must receive your application by 1 June. [9 words]

Political correctness — using political correctness often needs extra words to be spoken. The coded euphemisms, need de-coding by your audience (more cognitive load). Straightforward English is easier for your audience to understand and less likely to be misinterpreted.

Tautologies — The repetition of meaning, using different words. Just say things once! For example: added bonus — a bonus is an added extra (for example, extra pay) so expanding 'added bonus' results in 'added added extra'.

Don't give your audience extra work to do — keep their cognitive load to a minimum.

13.2　First impressions

Even if the audience already knows you, as you proceed to the podium, and speak your first few words, they are confirming, or forming, opinions about you. Once again, you can thank evolutionary biology — deciding quickly who is a friend or a foe is an important survival skill. We all do it.

There is much written about body language and the subject of the so-called 'non-verbal communication' is a huge field. So, just a few suggestions:

Stride out — In any aspect of your presentation that involves movement, locomote in a distinctive and confident way. This means a gait you are comfortable with, and shoes suitable for walking and standing. Stand as if you own the place, otherwise you signal *'I'm a victim - hit me'*. The corporate thugs don't need much encouragement to be nasty.

Dress code — All organisations have a dress code. Often these codes are not written down, but exist tacitly. How you dress at your presentation is an element of the first impression, so it is worth discovering what those secret norms are. Not following the dress code identifies you as an outsider. (Although in some cases this can be advantageous.)

13.3　Opening the presentation

The opening moment has two main functions, both are important:

Tune-in — Let's assume you are a stranger to the venue and the audience. With your first words, the audience are busy adjusting how they hear and listen to you. Everyone has an accent (the melody of speech) and a dialect (the words and grammar). The acoustic qualities of the venue (echo, attenuation, latency, and the ambient noise). Your audience need a few moments to adjust their internal tone controls and tune-in.

You also need a moment to tune-in to the same environment, but in the opposite direction. In the first few moments you'll be unconsciously modifying how you speak and adjusting your tone and pace to match the venue's acoustics. Give yourself time to do this — it takes just a few seconds and a few words.

So what?

Since reliable communication between you and the audience cannot be assumed during the first moments. It is wise not include any critical or important information in the first few seconds. Instead, offer salutations, thanks, and the like. Or if you're going straight for a big-bang start, design and rehearse the opening sentences so that the audience has time to tune-in.

> Remember: do not present any critical or important information in the first few seconds or minutes. There is a high risk of it becoming lost as you and your audience tune-in to one another.

Gain attention — The second job in the opening moments is to gain credibility. This is not the beginning of your story arc, but about you as the presenter. It is your personal introduction.

Table 9: Example of a personal introduction

Purpose	Example — spoken
① Salutation — to tune-in	① Good afternoon, thanks for the invitation, I'm delighted to be here.
② Asking for permission to use the audiences' time. Respecting Humanity. (Audience tuned-in.)	② My name is Alan; please let me introduce myself:
③ To gain credibility	③ I'm a chartered engineer...
④ Supporting facts, i) Experience (40 years), ii) Hard science subject. Iii) Polymath	④ ... from way back in 1980, originally as an electronic engineer in telecoms. And more recently in quality systems and business change.
⑤ One more thing. A tease, ask me later.	⑤ My claim to fame is a project transforming back-office teams (more than 600 people, with a budget exceeding £48m) from an overhead into valued business entities.
⑥ I'm well organised. 30 minutes 18 slides	⑥ Now, we have 30 minutes for this slot, and I have 18 slides. So, let's get started.
⑦ Respecting Humanity: Involving the audience. (Audience now checkin their pens..)	⑦ There is time for Q&A, but if you need me to return to a specific slide it would be really helpful if you could keep a note of the slide number in the lower-left corner. Thanks
⑧ Promise of a gift (the handout) Humanity: involve Lucy.	⑧ There are some handouts to take home. These are available from Lucy after the presentation. Lucy, if you'd just give a wave so everyone knows who you are. Thanks.

The whole introduction, delivered at a steady pace is about 30 to 45 seconds. If you're well known to the audience, this can be truncated to ①, ⑥, ⑦, (and ⑧ if relevant) and aim for 20 seconds. If you really want it short and sweet, go for just ①, ②, and ③. Mix and match until feels right.

> Always give yourself and your audience time to tune-in.

If you use more than about a minute, your audience might form the view that you are busy talking about yourself and polishing your ego, and with that comes their perception of your arrogance,

And now you're ready to commence your presentation with the story-arc.

14 Working with rogue behaviours

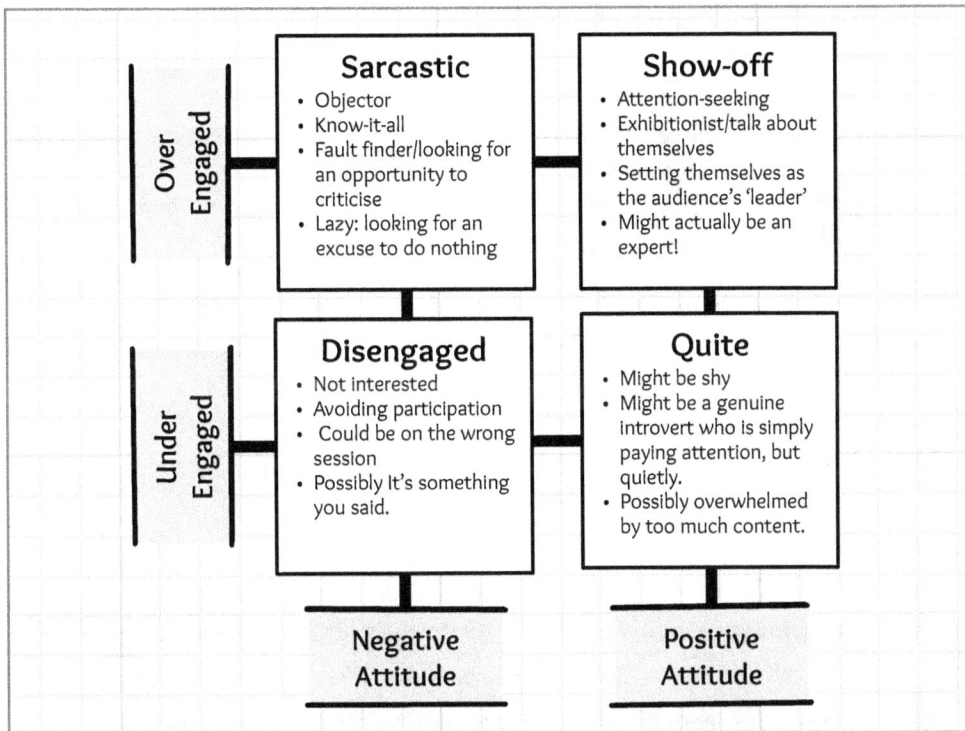

Figure 42: Understanding the rogue behaviour.

Not everything runs smoothly, and occasionally some members of the audience can make your job difficult. These behaviours come in many forms, Figure 42 shows a classification of behaviours based on the two dimensions of attitude and engagement. The 'sarcastic' and 'show-off' states can be disruptive both to you and the other participants. The 'disengaged' and 'quiet' states might cause you to wonder whether you've been doing something wrong.

14.1   Interventions for distractions

Most interventions require more questioning skills. For the distracters, the questions are more likely to be coaching questions, a type of directing question specifically framing a topic, and giving the responsibility for resolution to the distracter.

> Remember Mr Churchill's famous quip:
> *"Diplomacy is the ability to tell someone to go to hell in such a way that they look forward to the trip."*

Dealing with distracting behaviour is a critical moment to display your role model unconditionally positive attitude, and to avoid the negatives such as criticism or sarcasm.

Depending on the level of interaction you have with your audience; tactics such as the following help can help.

Back to the point/relevance — refer back to the presentation objective, and do a quick one-two: *"...an interesting point Harriet, just help us all out a little; how does reorganising the sales team help us with time management?"* (If you use this technique; use a quizzical tone of voice.) The response could go two ways: an elaborate explanation, or oops, it doesn't. For the elaborate explanation, your response is to bring Harriet, and hence the group, back to the point: *"... we cannot reorganise the sales team today, we can develop our time management skills..."* If it is still a problem (remember you can ask the participants), put the issue of a sales reorganisation on the Car Park/Issues Board.

Thank them for their help — acknowledge the intervention, thanking them for their input. Mention that you'll check with them at the end of each session. Convert them into a resource; speak to them during intervals to check that everything is going well.

Ask the audience — for example: *"Mike has said xyz, what do others think?"* Depending on how the audience reacts, invite more input by focusing on relevance: "Is Mike's point relevant to our topic today?" If it is interesting but not relevant: *"Shall we put Mike's point on the issues board?"*

Create guardian role — giving participants a specific role can accommodate distractors, or give the under-participating learners a reason to join in. There are many roles: being the scribe (but not timekeeper), summariser, counter (count all mentions of 'customer'), task analyser — for example, after a key message has been met, ask the distractor: *"Freda, would you think about the key tasks we should perform to support the <goal>?"* Then come back to it in the review.

A quiet word — speaking with a participant during the breaks often helps, and there are many reasons why a quite conversation is more advantageous than a (potentially) confrontational exchange in plenary. Having a quiet chat with a shy, quiet person, you might discover that they are perfectly fine and happy to listen, they might be a strong reflector and waiting for their moment. They might want a specific point covered but are afraid to ask. At least with a quiet chat you'll know.

The other need for a quiet conversation behind the scenes is with disruptive participants. Removing the audience (the other participants) means that there is no audience to play to. The distracter cannot play for status because there is no audience to provide it. You'll need to use coaching-style questions such as: *"Is this presentation meeting your needs?"* You'll get some answer. Build on it. Stronger questions might be: *"How are your interventions helping this agenda/session/the other participants?"* You'll get an answer. Ultimately you might end up with: *"It sounds as if this session isn't for you — would you like to leave?"* Then shake hands and help them to leave quickly and quietly (without an audience), before you reconvene the group.

Many other techniques exist and would fill another book!

15 Get ready — the floor is yours

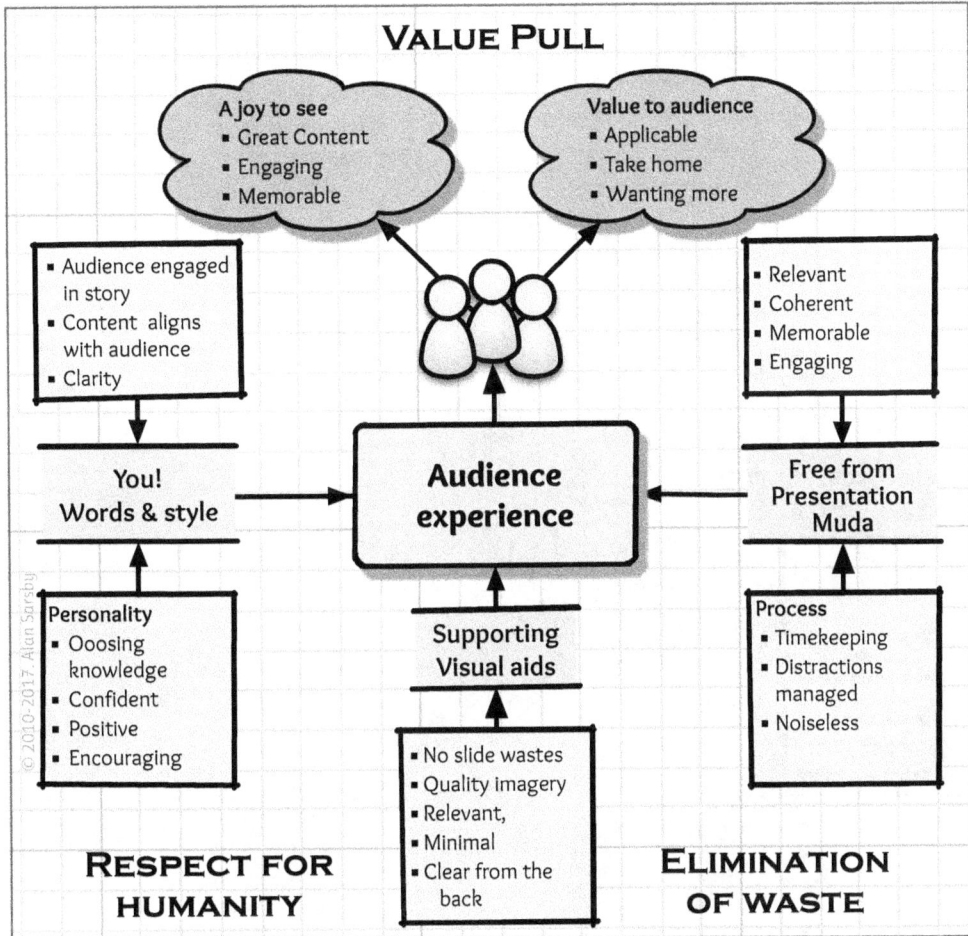

VALUE PULL

A joy to see
- Great Content
- Engaging
- Memorable

Value to audience
- Applicable
- Take home
- Wanting more

- Audience engaged in story
- Content aligns with audience
- Clarity

- Relevant
- Coherent
- Memorable
- Engaging

You!
Words & style

Audience experience

Free from Presentation Muda

© 2010-2017 Alan Sarsby

Personality
- Ooosing knowledge
- Confident
- Positive
- Encouraging

Supporting Visual aids

Process
- Timekeeping
- Distractions managed
- Noiseless

- No slide wastes
- Quality imagery
- Relevant,
- Minimal
- Clear from the back

RESPECT FOR HUMANITY

ELIMINATION OF WASTE

Figure 43: Everything in place for presentation delivery.

15.1   Design the delivery

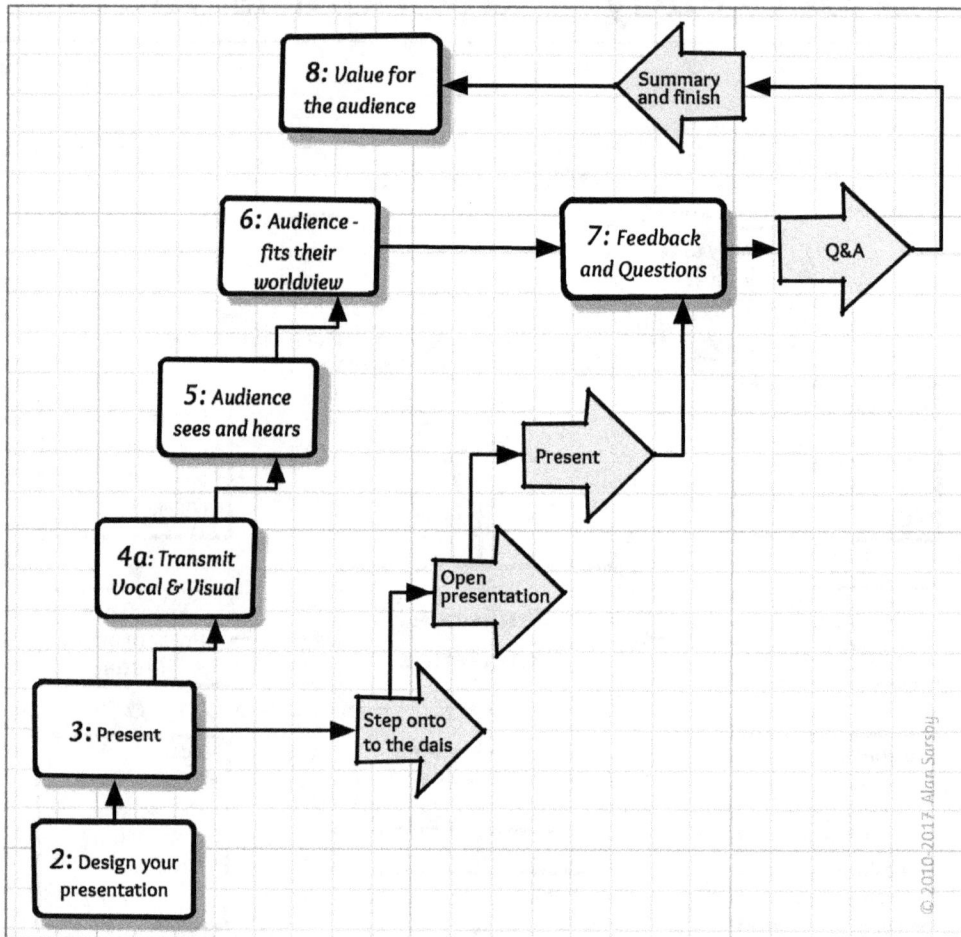

Figure 44: Delivering the presentation.

It might seem obvious by now, but the the delivery of your presentation also needs designing. And then tested through rehearsals and refinements. Figure 43 gives an overview of everything involved. A variation of Figure 4 is shown on the previous page in Figure 44.

Step up

There are many places you can deliver you presentation. On a dais, at a lectern/podium, or just by standing around a conference table.

When it is your moment to step up. Do so with straightforward competence and confidence.

Opening

There are many openings to choose from, using the story-arc helps a great deal.

Pace and rhythm

Pace is the speed that your orate your words; rhythm is the inflection you give your words—so you don't sound monotonic. The effectiveness of your spoken delivery follows a pace that ensures your audience can understand you, and the rhythm is making the listening easy. High-speed pace changes your words into gibberish. And no rhythm makes your voice into a monotonic dirge.

Your emotions

Remember you are a human. Humans have emotions, and emotions are often what defines and drives us. Unless you have the driest subject in the world let your emotions join in the presentation. Which leads to ...

Gesticulations

Gesticulations are part of our way of communicating. They range from a sweeping arm depicting a range or a swathe; to a kind of karate-chop favoured by politicians who want to appear decisive.

People can see you so gesticulations are good, and help define you as a person rather than an automaton. And hence ...

Converse

People listen to another people, or for a presenter a person. There is no such thing as a group listen. An audience of twenty people comprises twenty individual listenings, each listening for the things that matter to themselves. When planning and delivering the spoken word try to say it as a conversation with an individual or a friend. Look at one person for a moment whilst you deliver a line of speech, then move to another one, and so on around the room.

If you speak to only one person, the others have a choice to disengage. Once your audience tunes into this conversation-mode, they have to pay attention and engage because you might just ask a question and they'll be caught napping.

Conversations are generally between two people so use first and second-person forms of address. For example, *"your project"*, *Have you considered ...*, *"Our deadline is looming, ..."*, *"We have a surprise input..."*.
If you use the third person, especially 'they' in a passive voice, it is easy for the audience to disengage because no one knows who the imaginary 'they' is.

Owning the space

Wherever you are presenting from, it is your space. Don't pace about like an expectant father[1], but likewise there is no need to stand rigidly behind the lectern or behind your laptop. Stepping away means the audience can see you without intervening barriers. This invites the question ...

Where to stand?

Obviously, you don't want to block your audiences' view of the screen. So standing somewhere else is a good idea. Generally, we read from left-to-right, so standing on the left means that your audience reads you first, then the screen second.

Controlling the slides

If you're standing in the right place, you might be some distance away from your laptop. And that makes a remote control a necessity.

---

1   Expectant father — an idiom. Arising from traditional births where the mother-to-be, the midwife, and nurses (traditionally, all female) are busy in the hospital ward (or in the bedroom) and the menfolk are excluded. The father stressfully paces up and down whilst nervously waiting for the birth to happen.

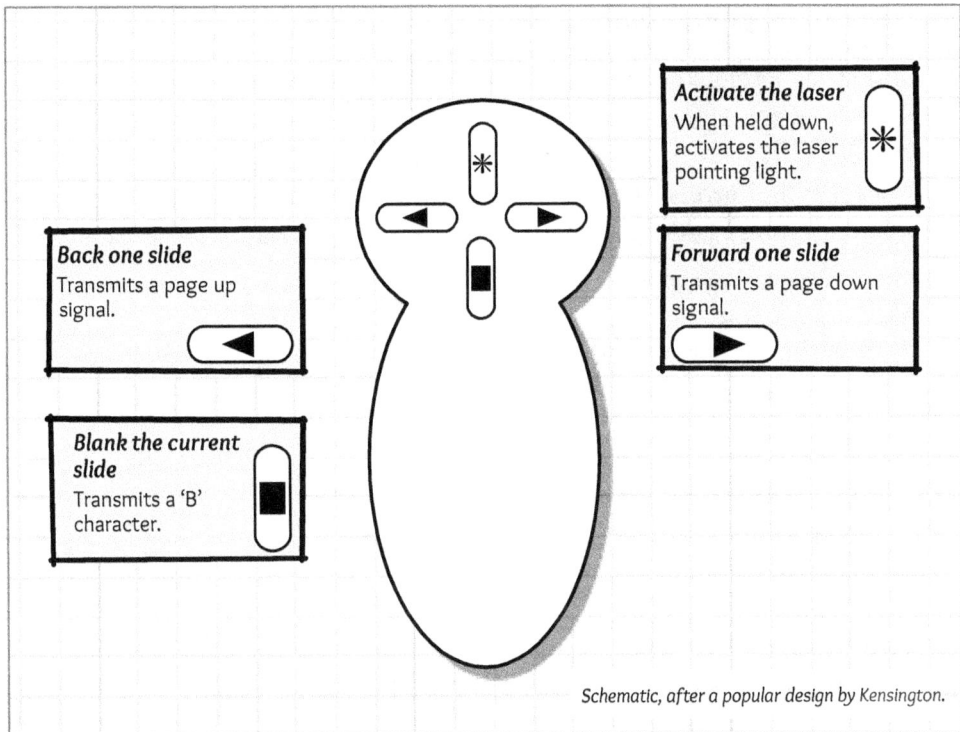

Activate the laser
When held down, activates the laser pointing light.

Back one slide
Transmits a page up signal.

Forward one slide
Transmits a page down signal.

Blank the current slide
Transmits a 'B' character.

Schematic, after a popular design by Kensington.

Figure 45: A remote control (clicker).

Choose a remote that fits your hand. You can operate the remote discreetly rather than waving it around. There's no need to zap/shoot the remote to the screen/computer for operation!

The most underused key is the 'B' button. There are situations where you might be speaking about is unrelated to what is on screen. This is contrary to the *Effective Redundancy* design principle — and you're creating an opportunity for failure. Your audience are listening to you, but watching something else — confusion! Noise! Waste! It is a situation that makes it easy for your audience to disengage.

> If you're wondering, the B key causes the software to display a black screen, and similarly, the W key displays a white screen. This works in both Powerpoint and Keynote.

> To move to a specific slide, simply type the number followed by ENTER. Depending on your software and version, the presentation jumps to that slide, or presents a light box/slide sorter view and you select from there. (Hence the importance of numbering your slides.)

15.2   Rehearse and Revise

Rehearsing has several important benefits. Among these are:

Timing

It seems that there is little correlation between the number of slides and the length of time a presentation takes. I'm sure you can recall presenters with only five slides and taking an hour to do it.

A rehearsal gives an indication of your duration.

Flow

Your audience are likely to think better of you if you can deliver your presentation in an articulated and confident manner. Your own rehearsal exposes where the story arc stumbles and hence the need for revision.

Your Voice

Speaking aloud your presentation helps you to train your voice. Think of an actor learning their lines. Learning your lines means that you can dispense with clumsy notes.

How you pitch your voice depends on the purpose and desired outcome. Hard or aggressive tones are appropriate to some story-arcs: cold and factual, we're in trouble, but are not suitable for encouragement and celebrations. Similarly light, inflective, tones are encouraging, and support learning oriented presentations. And inappropriate for grave and serious matters.

How to rehearse

The dry run

Book a conference room and set everything up as it would be for the real event. Then present to an empty room. When you are more confident, invite a friendly audience.

Video yourself

Even videoing yourself at the dry run is helpful. You'll soon discover how often you use filler words, the 'like' and the frustrating "you know what I mean". You'll discover where you are using the *grunts ums* and *errs*. With rehearsals, those grunts become less because you don't need the thinking time and consequently the flow becomes better.

Ask a mentor

A friendly mentor is useful because they are often the only person who can give you the feedback you need.

> Your boss might not be a suitable mentor. Help from your boss might end up with you giving the presentation that the boss would like to give: then it is not your presentation!

Ruthless editing

After the first rehearsal, you'll discover where your presentation needs editing. You'll need to be decisive: If the point is straying from the story arc, either edit to put it back, or cut it. If the flow is faltering, edit to reinstate the flow.

16 Questions

16.1   Using questions in the presentation

Questions are a good form of engagement. They come in many forms, each with a distinct purpose.

Table 10: Questions in presentations.

Type of question	Examples	When to use
Closed	May I just check, are you all engineers?	Use as warm-up questions where the answers are simple and safe.
Open	Hi, how are things?	Small group presentations to invite participation. More difficult in large groups.
Directing (semi-open)	Tell me more about your presentation problems.	Signals to the audience that you want them to give you more information about *xyz*, and by implication, not *abc*. Then follow up with further questions that draw out key points. Requires the participant to *think*, rather than recall. (Good for presentations to small groups.)
Leading (semi-closed)	This is a clever solution, isn't it?	It is a type of closed question that requires the participant to agree with you. You are putting your words into the mouth of the audience. Use this type of question with extreme care.
Rephrasing	So, what you're saying is ...?	To convert the audience's language into the language of the subject matter. To guide an unstructured response into a form that supports the point.
Provocative	On an electric plug, What happens if the brown and blue wires are reversed?	To test for a deeper understanding of the subject. Requires thinking. (In this case there are several correct answers.) Good for an intellectual activity.

The questions can be on-slides or spoken as a voice-over. Remember the earlier point that a presentation overloaded with questions becomes a exhausting cognitive load for the audience, so use them wisely.

16.2   Receiving questions in the Q&A session.

The Question/Answer session can be a stressful moment: You have no idea what is coming next, and the need to think on your feet is suddenly very important.

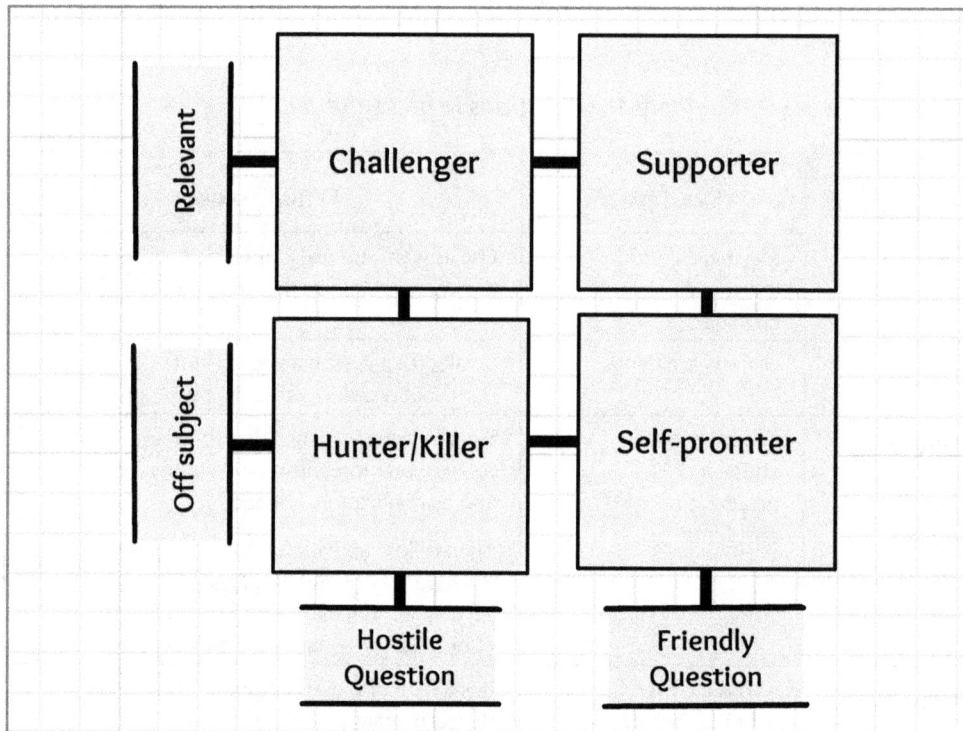

Figure 46: Analysis of question types.

The supporter

How to identify the supporter — supporters are often enthusiastic and thank you profusely for your very interesting presentation.

How to respond with the supporters — Thank them for their generous feedback (this alone encourages other latent supporters to step up to the microphone). Perhaps ask where they see a use for the topic. Invite your supporters to seek you out at the coffee break.

The self promoter

How to identify the self-promoter — this group often start their question with gushing praise but swiftly change tack into talking about themselves and how wonderful they are. In fact they are pitching for business or status on the back of your presentation. They are not asking you a question, but borrowing your glory to speak to the audience.

How to respond to the self-promoter — Interrupt them mid-flow: *"er, yes, Anne thanks for the feedback, In the interest of looking after our time budget, do you have a specific question?"* Probably they don't in which case a swift *"Thanks for your feedback; next question please."*

The challenger

How to identify the challenger — There are three forms of challengers:

- The genuine challengers who consider your logic is wrong, your assumptions are unsound, and so on.

- Those who are basically negative or mischievous.

- Those who disagree with anything.

How to respond to the challenger — the first group, the genuine challengers; thank them for their observation and reassure them that the material was reviewed prior to presentation. If you know people in their team, mention that their colleague was involved in the preparation to defuse their objection.

It might be the case that their challenge is correct and you've missed something. Be bold and admit it, offer to take it into consideration. Then, *"thanks for the observation, I'll follow it up off-line, and get back to you. Next question."* Keep the pace moving.

The Hunter/Killer loaded or trap question

How to identify the hunter/killer — these hunter/killers are often skilled in their attack. Politicians (those in politics, or those in organisations with a political culture) enjoy this behaviour. Its purpose is not to make themselves look good, but to enjoy making you look foolish.

Typical question formats include:

"Would you not agree that (trivial matter) and consequently xyz would be a better approach?

"You mention abc, but your conclusion does not necessarily follow. (Followed by a tenuous or far-fetched example.)

The alerting phrases are *"Would you not agree"* and *"not necessarily"*. Notice that both have a negative modifier. The trappers often add their solution/conclusion to their question.

How to respond to the trapper — you need to stick to your position and show some courage.

"No xyz is not relevant."

"I'm sure there are alternative approaches, but our proposal has been field-tested (a form of appeal to a higher authority) and has support from all our stakeholders."

Questions come in may forms so it is worth taking a moment to think about what you've been asked. If you think it helpful, play for time, and either, ask the questioner to repeat the question, or use the device of *"if I understand your question, you are asking about ... ."* And then answer your own interpretation of their question. Use a story arc to frame your answer.

16.3   Closing the Q&A

Contrary to popular belief and received wisdom, the Q&A is not the end of your presentation. The final word should be you speaking in your own voice. If you've had hostile questions, this is your moment to recover the high-ground, and finish by restating your purpose, successes, and what next. Many of the story arcs fit this moment, and with practice you can summarise your key points in a few seconds.

16.4   Final thoughts for questions

In the adrenaline charged moments of a presentation, it is easy to stumble. With that in mind, here are a few extras:

- Try not to start each answer with the preposition, 'So ...'

- Remember to respond to the point, not the person (even if the person is unpleasant). A variation on this is to handle the question, not the questioner.

- Reuse the story-arcs for your answer. Find a few favourites, become familiar with those and use them for a well-structured response. (And gain good vibes from your audience who admire your cool, calm, professionalism.)

- Be bold and interrupt questioners who are stealing your time and reputation. *"Thank you, blah, blah. Next question ..."* And be strict with those who just like the sound of their own voice and want to talk about themselves.

- If you genuinely can't answer a question, you have several escape routes: ask the audience (but do not relinquish control) ask a team member to pick up the question, *"Your question would be better answered by my team member, David."* (This has a powerful reputation enhancing affect: you trust your colleagues, and you publicly give credit for their talents and contributions.) You could also offer to meet the questioner at the next coffee break and offer to find out the answer.

Always honour the naïve question
Imagine that a participant has just realised an important point and asks a question; you have heard this question a hundred times in your experience. However, for the participant it is their first time, so respond to the participant with the same enthusiasm as if it were the first time you've heard it. You'll have the advantage of having a rehearsed answer, and you'll come across to your audience in a positive way.
Honouring the naïve question is a core behaviour of Respecting Humanity.

17 Working with feedback

Your presentation is over, and you're feeling good. Enjoy the moment.
Now, in the spirit of continuous improvement, the next job is feedback and a review.

Your personal post-presentation review

Your review is a form of reflection, which is looking back at what went well, and what might need changing. If you are naturally a reflector or a theorist this is a straightforward task; if you are an activist or pragmatist you'll need to step outside your zone and force yourself into reflector-mode. There are many ways of doing your personal review: quietly in your head, on sticky-notes on your desk or flipchart, as a list, or directly into presentation software if you intend to share it or use it again.

To get you started, use the presentation charter (Figure 8) and your story arc. Stepping through the slides often prompts your memory to recall particular moments. Typical points to cover might be:

- Was the presentation's purpose and objectives met?

- Was it was relevant for the audience?

- What definitely worked?

- What should be changed.

From your own review, identify what you could add to your personal development plan, or to your Continuing Professional Development (CPD) objectives?

A peer review with another presenter

Other presenters see and hear things that you might be unaware of; for example, each other's style and tone of delivery, observation of incidents whilst you happened to be looking elsewhere, and so on.

Customer (audience) feedback

Designing, collecting, and evaluating feedback is a non-trivial component of your presentation. It needs designing with the same dedication as the other elements of your work. Keep in mind that feedback is not free; there is work for you, but importantly work and cognitive load for your audience.

All your hard work in creating a fantastic presentation can be undone by a poor quality feedback session, which is both wasteful and reputation-destroying.

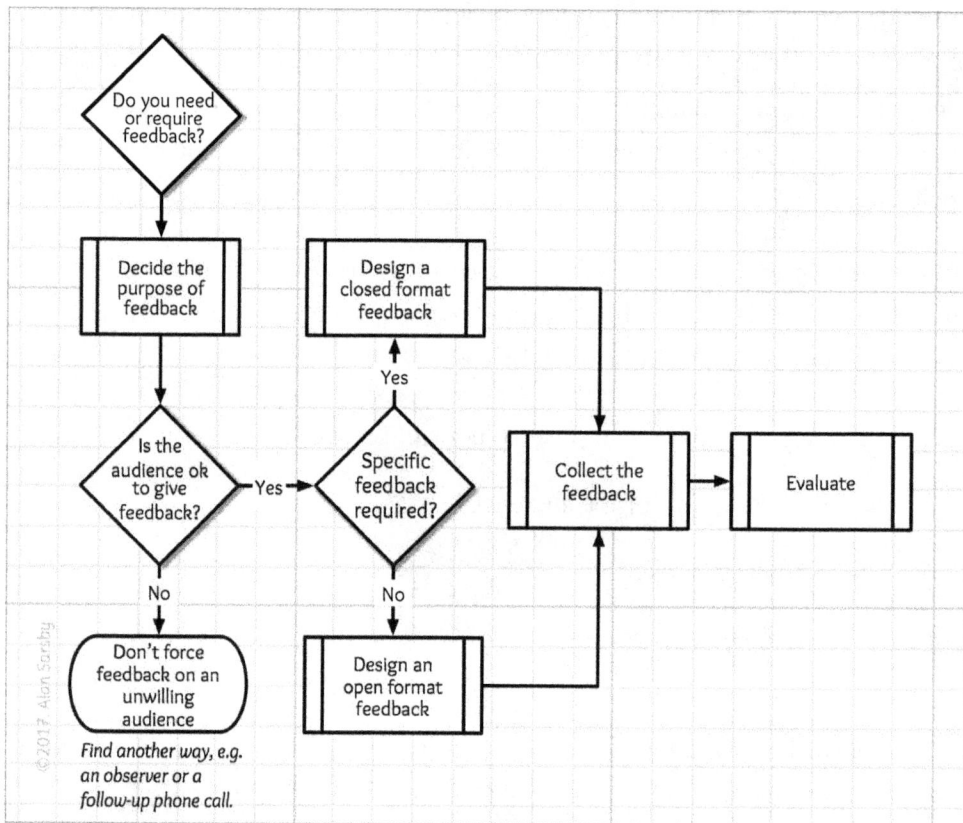

Figure 47: A skeletal plan for deciding and designing feedback.

Hint: Use the presentation charter (§4.3) as your design input.

Closed format — Closed format feedback involves designing directing questions which can be graduated from an audience's from *poor* to *great*. A scoring scheme from, say 1 — 5, makes it easy to process the responses in a spreadsheet to give an overall feedback score.

To make this approach successful, keep in mind:

- Choose directing questions, (§16).
  (Take extreme care not to ask leading questions.)

- Keep the cognitive load light. Aim for the fewest number of questions.

- Design relevant and worthwhile questions.

The biggest disadvantage with close format feedback is that you have to consider all possible elements of feedback and build those into your design. If your audience really wants to give an item of feedback and it is not on your list, they'll feel excluded. And your great presentation is spoilt by badly designed feedback.

Open format — Open format feedback invites the audience to respond by finishing two sentences beginning with *'I liked ...'* and *'I wish...'.* With suitable encouragement, you can harvest a very wide ranging set of issues. But, to make sense of them requires skilled processing to draw out themes and issues.

To make this approach successful, keep in mind:

- Encourage the audience by orating some simple examples that also demonstrate the value to you. For example:
  "I could ask you if you liked lunch, in the form of a tick-box, but If you answer with a 'no' then, I don't know what aspect of lunch to change. On the other hand, if you give me feedback such as 'I liked the fish' then I know it is a good decision for next time. If you say 'I wish the dish had garden peas instead of mushy' then I know to change the vegetables."

- Other guidance for your audience is to start with the *'I liked'* and all responses must be in a positive tone.

- "Design enough time for the audience to become engaged in the feedback, it is a heavy duty intellectual engagement activity.

Feedback can be both written or spoken. Figure 48 summarises closed/open with written/spoken feedback.

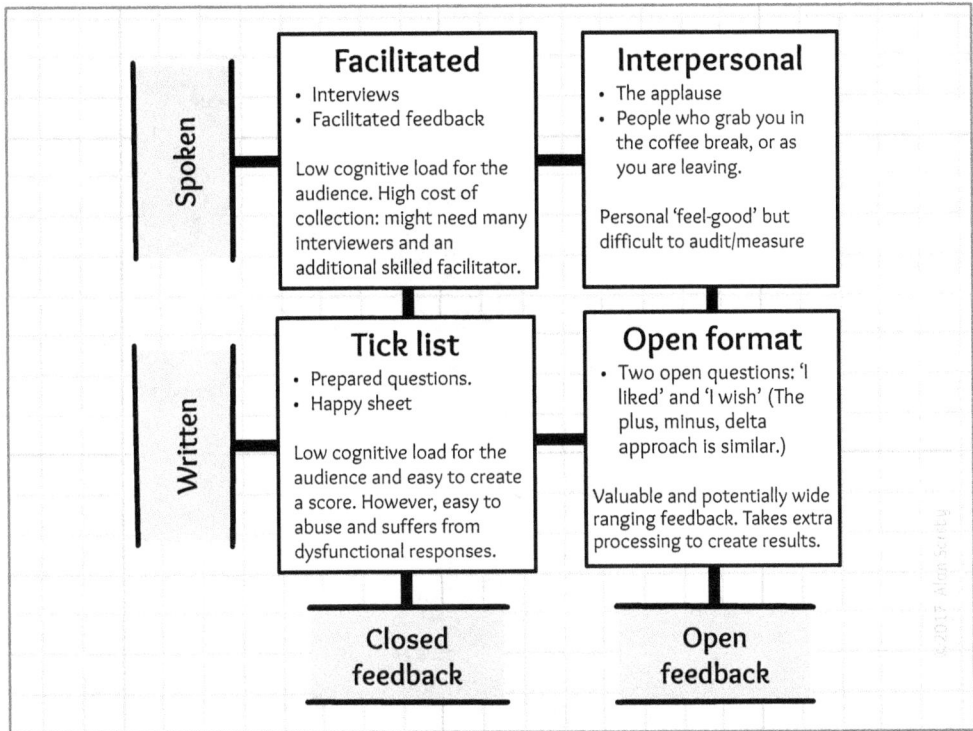

	Facilitated	Interpersonal
Spoken	• Interviews • Facilitated feedback Low cognitive load for the audience. High cost of collection: might need many interviewers and an additional skilled facilitator.	• The applause • People who grab you in the coffee break, or as you are leaving. Personal 'feel-good' but difficult to audit/measure
Written	**Tick list** • Prepared questions. • Happy sheet Low cognitive load for the audience and easy to create a score. However, easy to abuse and suffers from dysfunctional responses.	**Open format** • Two open questions: 'I liked' and 'I wish' (The plus, minus, delta approach is similar.) Valuable and potentially wide ranging feedback. Takes extra processing to create results.
	Closed feedback	**Open feedback**

Figure 48: Contrasting open/closed with written/spoken feedback formats

A review, or report, to your sponsor

The sponsor is also likely to require some feedback from your presentation. Try not to make assumptions, ask the sponsor what they would like to know. Normally this is a one-page document using the KISS principle (Keep It Short and Sweet). A minimal story arc for this type of report is something like: a summary of the objective, who was there, the budget consumed, achievement of the objectives, feedback, and any issues.

> Author's tip:
> Don't write an excessively long report; a busy sponsor won't appreciate it.

Appendix 1: Story arcs

1   Voyage of self discovery
Stable state — There is a problem — The problem is me. I must fix myself
— enlightenment —action. — Return as a new self.

2   The hero's mission
Once upon a time — a problem (an evil) — It needs a hero — I am not a hero —
but there is no one else — I must do it myself — Journey to eliminate the evil —
Overcome the obstacles — Win the fight — return as a real hero.

3   Past - Present - Future

4   Proposal, Pros, Cons, Decision.

5   SPIN: Situation, Problem, Impact, then ActioN

6   PREP - Position - Reason - Example - Position

- State your position, (core message)

- Give your reasons for it.

- Show a compelling example, and

- close by restating your position

7   Burning Bridge - No going back - New Future (also known as: Move-away-from, and move towards).

8   The Goldilocks Story

- Break the rule and explore forbidden territory (the woods),

- Adventure: the 'Just Right' story' not too much, not too little, but just right. Also known as the middle path story.

- Learning points (and reprimand 'if you had done as you were told to.').

9   Problem, Cause Solution, Benefits

10   Traffic light story:

- Red — Stop what we're doing.

- Amber — Prepare for something else.

- Green — Do this instead.

11   Pride and celebration.

12   Announcements:

- Welcomes,

- New Strategy. (Vision, Goals, Action)

- Is/is not examples.

13   Technical How-to. (Including Knowledge management).

14   One thing this week ... See Appendix 2. Good for impromptu presentations.

15   Marketing stories (N)AIDA

- Create a Need.

- Gain Attention,

- Generate an Interest,

- Convert to a Desire,

- Take Action.

16   Sales stories

- What is Need/Requirement

- Understand the benefits

- Make an Offer

- Overcome objections

- Make sale.

17   Omega
1) Theory. 2) Set up an activity. 3) Run the activity. 4 De-brief activity. 5 Review and learning points.
Useful if there is a training aspect.

18   Tell - Tell - Tell — Tell them what you're going to tell the audience. Tell it to the audience. Tell the audience what you told them, a summary. (Sometimes known as the BBC 9 o'clock news format).

19   Kolb learning cycle: 1) An experience, 2) Review of the experience, 3) Learning and generalisation, 4) Future: Apply the learning to new circumstances.
      Good for post-project reviews.

20   A Character - The struggle - Achievement of a goal.

21   Ideal World - Real World - What is the problem - This is the Solution - Next Steps. (A variation is known as the Knowing-Doing gap.)

22   Jenson's 5 Questions[1]: Relevance, What should I do (audience), Consequences and measures, What tools and support, WIIFM? (What's In It For Me?)

23   Chronological narrative (the crime scene story).
      Variations include children's' stories 'Once upon a time' . The Biblical equivalent is 'And it came to pass.' Take care with these because they don't have fixed starting points (date/time) and can be perceived as not grounded in reality.

24   Lessons learnt - especially good after a project finishes, or after a crisis. Structure as a short SPIN with extra elements of reflection so it becomes SPINL.

25   DMAIC. As a story. D) What was the Problem. M) How much of a problem (measure). A) Make sense of the problem. I) Eliminate the problem C) Embed the solution into business as usual.

---

1   Simplicity.Jenson, Bill. ISBN 978 0006532170

Appendix 2: Six stories to avoid

I want to Tell-you-All-I-know — The danger with telling everything you know about the topic, is that it results in too much content. You'll probably loose your audience with information overload and overrun the session time.

If you find yourself preparing an all-I-know presentation, be sure that you're not stroking your own ego.

Stick to the discipline of matching the level of your material to the level of the audience. Use a story arc to keep the pace moving and remove the waste content.

The party bag presentation — A presentation made up of of loosely related miscellaneous points. This is often a trap when you're required to give a 'topical' presentation with very short notice. What often happens is that you raid other presentations to create a mishmash of a presentation without a purpose nor a story arc.

The ideal way to deal with these is just to say 'thanks, but no thanks'. If you really have to give a presentation use the *'One Thing this week'* approach. For example *"The one thing that's {bothering me} {worked really well} this week is ..."*; then use a simple story arc. This approach lends itself to a well-structured ad lib, and avoids the need for any slides.

The shot by its own bullets presentation — These are popular with lazy presenters who simply list bullet after bullet points. Sometimes there is a structure with the slide heading providing much-needed orientation for the audience. However the real use for these is to act as a crib sheet for the presenter who speaks incoherently using the bullets as a aide-memoir.

There isn't any value for the audience, so it breaks both key principles of Lean: no respect nor value for the audience, and the Six-Sigma 5S principle of 'set in order' is lost.

To cure your laziness, try a self-training period where you don't use bullet points. Then start again with a well structured Lean presentation. Otherwise, do the world a favour and just don't give presentations. Thanks.

The Eddy presentation — In science and engineering, an Eddy is a turbulent flow, typically fluidic such as the swirl left in the water after a boat's oars are lifted, or a magnetic flux circulating in a ferrite core as the main flux encounters impurities. An Eddy presentation is full of personal anecdotes used by the presenter to support some point; it often takes some time for these 'stories' and metaphors to appear relevant which confuses your audience. In engineering, Eddy currents are a source of energy loss; energy loss is a waste. Elimination of waste is a core principle of Lean. Therefore eliminate the Eddy currents.

Eddy presentations are overcome by planning and design, then honed by rehearsals, so that you end up with a story board without the Eddies.

The Supermarket Dash presentation — This is based on a television quiz show: the prize for the winning contestant would be a supermarket dash. The dash is a timed visit, typically two-minutes, to the supermarket to run along the aisles placing (often throwing/scooping!) groceries into the trolly. The winner then keeps all items in the trolly. (And as you might guess, contestants gamed the event by heading directly for the high-value shelfs such as wine and spirits.)

The dash is characterised by running out of time. The audience is treated to phrases such as:

- *"We've only got a minute so I'll keep it short."*
  (Under-promise and Under-deliver.)

- *"This topic needs a lot more time, so I'll do the brief version."*
  (You're not worth the full version.)

- *"I've run out of time so I'll stop there."*
  (Abandon the audience.)

The dash can be eliminated by the mantra and action — 'Rehearse and Revise' so that the timing and content fit together within the overall time-slot.

The Get-to-the-point presentation — The audience have invested their time and had it wasted with excessive sections on 'who we are', 'our history' 'methodology' and such like, before getting to the point of the presentation. This is often used by a speaker who must say something, but doesn't have anything to say.

If you haven't anything to say (see §2.2), decline the offer to give a presentation. (Refer to the *Foreword*. Save the electrons, save the energy, save global warming.

Appendix 3: Learning styles

Learning theories

Understanding a little about learning styles theory is useful because it has a direct impact on presentation design and delivery.

> Author's note: There is a great deal of academic controversy about learning styles. This book is a guide, so we're going to be economical with the theory.

The term for the science of learning by adults is andragogy — roughly meaning man leading. Malcolm Knowles[1] developed the theory and offered six presuppositions for why andragogy is different from pedagogy.

- Adults need to know WHY they are learning something.

- Experience (including mistakes) is the basis for learning activities.

- Adults are responsible for their decisions regarding learning.

- Adults are most interested in learning that has immediate relevance to their lives (work-related or elsewhere).

- Learning is by problem solving.

- Adults respond better to internal motivators (self-interest — what is in it for them), rather than external motivators.

These all have an impact on presentation design and delivery.

There are approximately seventy models of learning styles, we'll take a look at just one.

---

1   ibid p 30.

Honey and Mumford Learning styles

The one learning styles model we are going to cover is that developed by Peter Honey and Alan Mumford[1]. Their model identifies four distinct preferences for adult learning. These learning preferences are highly relevant because they impact the structure and sequence of training delivery. Abbreviated descriptions of the four Honey and Mumford learning styles are:

Activist

Participants who prefer to learn by doing something are activists. Frequently they are not interested in the theory, and live in the 'here and now' moment. Once the activity has delivered its purpose, they become disinterested and are ready to move on.

Impact: the presentation should include activities. The activity depends on the number of people in your audience, and whether they are sat at a desk. Activities might include puzzles that can be solved using pen/paper, or some recollection. (Although activists, generally, prefer a hands-on, rather than intellectual, activity.)

Pragmatist

Pragmatists become interested in the topic if they can see how it might be put to use after your presentation. Honey and Mumford describe these participants as 'down to earth' and additionally characterise pragmatists "as long as it works, that's fine".
(By the way, this often annoys the theorists*.)

Impact: the introduction to a topic should identify the benefit and application of the subject-matter and learning to the real world before delivering the content. Pragmatists are impatient, so you should get to the point quickly.

Theorist

As the descriptor suggests, theorists prefer to understand the principles before moving on to using them. Theorists learn by logic and deduction, cause and effect, and models that hold a topic together.

---

1   Honey, P and Mumford, A (1992), The manual of learning styles, Peter Honey Publications.

Impact: In the story-arc, you need to present the theory elements before an activity or application. If you jump straight into the detail, the theorists will find it difficult to engage. To them, the theory must come first.

> (*) Theorists don't accept the approach of pragmatists who can arrive at the right answer using the wrong methods or faulty logic. If the Pragmatists and Theorists start arguing (which they often do) you may need to undertake some crowd control!

Reflector

For the reflectors, the learning only consolidates when they have had the opportunity to look back on what has been presented and what has happened. Reflectors prefer to stand back, and observe and think before being satisfied with the topic.

Impact: At the end of a topic, it is essential to devote time to review the subject, summarise the points, and encourage the reflectors to be involved. If you are running out of time, don't be tempted to ditch the summary (especially if your personal learning preference is activist or pragmatist).

Sequence of delivery

The Honey and Mumford learning styles suggest a sequence for your story arc and especially when designing and planning your presentation.

This sequence is:

- Introduce the purpose and relevance of the presentation subject topic. This satisfies the Knowles andragogic requirement for an adult to know *why* they should pay attention.

- Explain the benefits and uses to which the subject-matter can be used in the workplace. This keeps the pragmatists satisfied for the time being, and fulfils the Knowles requirement for immediate relevance.

- Deliver the supporting theory building up from component parts to a logical whole. This satisfies the theorists, so they can now participate in an activity (otherwise, the activity is wasted on them).

- Do an activity. An activity satisfies both the activists and pragmatists. A well-designed activity also satisfies the theorists' need to apply and test the theory (hence, the importance of explaining the aim or objectives of the activity); and the reflectors need to observe how it works. An activity meets the Knowles requirements for experience and problem solving.

- Finish the presentation with a review or a summary. This satisfies the reflectors and consolidates the theorists. It meets the Knowles requirement for adults owning their own learning, and the satisfaction of internal motivation.

- Summarise the presentation messages.

Appendix 4: The magic lantern

A little history — The original projector was the Magic Lantern. It worked by the operator sliding glass-based images along a smooth track into the lantern's optical path — hence 'slides'. The terminology carried over to 35mm photography where images were recorded onto a transparent film coated with a light sensitive emulsion. When processed correctly a 'positive' image is created rather than a negative. These were known as Diapositives or reversal film because during processing the 'negative' was reversed into a positive image, which could then be projected by placing the diapositive (slide) between a light source and an optical transmission train. The main advantage of diapositives is that many people (the audience) could see the image at the same time, instead of passing prints around the room.

The modern version of a magic lantern is the digital projector it is driven by the graphic output of a computer. Anything that can appear on the computer screen, can be projected to the screen[1]. With the popularity of digital projectors, the terminology has changed. In current parlance, the term slide has is being replaced by Projected Digital Image (PDI), or occasionally Digital Projected Image (DPI). However, the two popular presentation software tools; Apple's Keynote, and Microsoft's PowerPoint, the term *slide* is still used.

In a digital age, it is odd to think of a projected image as a 'slide'. As a verb, *to slide* means to move smoothly along a surface. With the invention of the Magic Lantern, the term slide became part of the presentation vocabulary.

---

1   A small condition must be added to the statement: If you are projecting via a HDMI connection, it is worth noting that the HDMI protocols include license-management functions that can trigger the HDMI connexion to block the video stream to the projector. This depends on the copyright codes in the source file.
For more information visit: en.wikipedia.org/wiki/High-bandwidth_Digital_Content_Protection/

Figure 49: An early Magic Lantern.

The images were mounted in a carrier which slides through a bracket to a position behind the lens. See the image credits for more information.

Slide-shows became popular from the early 1800s. Even as presentations, the magic lantern pre-dates modern software by several hundreds of years.

Figure 50: A presentation using a magic lantern.

Appendix 5: Your computer

Is your laptop powerful enough?

If you embed video in your presentation, choose a computer (often a laptop) which is powerful enough to project via the video-out port to the projector. You might see it work correctly on-screen at your desk, but driving a projector requires more powerful graphics performance.

Kit bag

If you're travelling with your own laptop and projector and you've tested it throughly one could reasonably assume it is going to work on the day.

But, if you're using someone else's projector, make sure you take a full complement of adaptors to meet any form of audio visual connector you might encounter. Be aware some might be old or obsolete, especially if you're going to a 'budget-constrained' environment.

A note about your file

Portable computers have a low tolerance for falling off conference room tables, or being catapulted across the room when someone trips over the power cord. If you are dependent on your computer to project a file, consider carrying various types of backup on a memory stick:

- A copy of your file (.ppt/.pptx or .key)—it may be possible to run your presentation from someone else's computer. This assumes they have a compatible version of the application software and have the same fonts on their system as those used in your presentation.

- Depending on your software, you might also save your presentation as web pages or as a series of images. You can then use an internet browser to display the images.

- Export your presentation in the Portable Document Format (.pdf). Almost every computer can read and display portable documents. Simply put your pdf reader into full-screen mode and present from that. You'll lose the fancy transitions and animations, but no harm in that!

- Remember to embed your fonts in the pdf; that way whatever font you've used (say a corporate font[1]), it is projected correctly.

- Embed images, rather than linking to them.

> Author's note: Important presentations and budget laptops are not good companions. If your laptop throws up an error message as you start your presentation to a hundred-person audience, it can be embarrassing and disruptive.
>
> This opportunity for failure is easily identified in a full dress rehearsal to reveal these problems in advance.

---

1   Note that fonts can only be embedded if they are licensed to do that. Embedding is controlled by settings inside the font file.

Acknowledgements

All diagrams © the author, except as follows.

Figure 29 — © Dr. Jos Harris. From:
Liquid micro-junction surface sampling and MALDI imaging of small and large molecules in human liver disease, University of Birmingham, September 2015. Used with permission.

Figure 49, Author: Lomita (Own work)
Title: Lanterne magique; 19 April 2015.
License: [CC BY-SA 4.0 (http://creativecommons.org/licenses/by-sa/4.0)]

Figure 50 — © The Magic Lantern Society 2007. All rights reserved.
www.magiclantern.org.uk/
Downloaded: 2017-05-16 from www.magiclantern.org.uk/images/zahn2.jpg
Used as per their requirements documented at http://www.magiclantern.org.uk/copyright.html
Verified: 2017-11-16

About the author

Alan Sarsby has enjoyed over forty years in varied careers, initially in electronic engineering, and IT strategy. Then in customer service and business change. He has developed and implemented novel approaches to enterprise design and change leadership. In 2001, he established is own company specialising in training services. He is a conference speaker and non-fiction author.

Alan has many years' experience as a leadership trainer in blue-chip organisations. He is an expert in project leadership including the many associated tools which of-course, include the ability to influence and update stakeholders through effective presentation techniques.

Alan may be able to help you with:

- Training, workshops and seminars, conference speaking.

- Consulting services.

- Customised versions of this of this book to incorporate your own organisation's policies.

Contact: email to editor@leadership-library.co.uk

A dedicated web page is here: www.leanpresentations.uk including updates and blog articles.

Your feedback

If this book has helped with your presentation, we'd be delighted if you'd let us know. Alternatively, consider posting a review on the site where you obtained this book.

If you have suggested improvements, it would be good to know those too. And if you have ideas for similar subject matter, please send an email. Thanks.

Good luck with your presentation.

—Δ—

www.ingramcontent.com/pod-product-compliance
Lightning Source LLC
Chambersburg PA
CBHW051217200326
41519CB00025B/7155